How to Survive Your Viva

How to Survive Your Viva

Defending a thesis in an oral examination

Rowena Murray

Open University Press

Open University Press
McGraw-Hill Education
McGraw-Hill House
Shoppenhangers Road
Maidenhead
Berkshire
England
SL6 2QL

email: enquiries@openup.co.uk
world wide web: www.openup.co.uk

and Two Penn Plaza, New York, NY 10121-2289, USA

First published 2009

A catalogue record of this book is available from the British Library

ISBN-13: 978-0-33-523382-3 (pb)
ISBN-10: 0-33-523382-1 (pb)

Library of Congress Cataloguing-in-Publication Data
CIP data applied for

Typeset by RefineCatch Limited, Bungay, Suffolk
Printed in the UK by Bell and Bain Ltd, Glasgow

Fictitious names of companies, products, people, characters and/or data that may be used herein (in case studies or in examples) are not intended to represent any real individual, company, product or event.

The **McGraw·Hill** Companies

This book is dedicated to

The village people (Lochwinnoch and Brig O' Turk)

Contents

Preface

Origins of this book

This is the first book of its kind to be published in the UK. It builds on the success of my video on *The Viva* and draws on years of viva and supervision workshops, discussions with students, supervisors and examiners, plus current research on the viva. This second edition provides an update on more recent research.

For all disciplines

While the focus is the doctoral examination, this book is intended to be relevant to all disciplines and to all forms of doctorate requiring an oral examination.

Upgrades and transfers

There is material here that will help those facing MPhil upgrades and other oral examinations.

Variations in practice

It is important to signal right from the start of this book that in cultures where there are significant variations in practice, such as the UK, the onus is on students, supervisors and examiners to check local procedures and to consider how – or even whether or not – to apply the advice offered in this book in specific contexts.

This process of checking is prompted throughout this book in boxes. These boxes identify specific issues for readers to follow up at their own institutions.

What's wrong with the doctoral examination?

Many authors set out to define what is wrong with the doctoral examination, in the UK in particular, most indicating what researchers and practitioners consider should be done to 'fix' it. Yet there has not yet been a full treatment of how to manage the viva as it presently exists. If it were better managed, if students and examiners were better prepared and if there were more transparency about what actually happens 'behind closed doors', it might be less intimidating and more educational.

Talking about writing

Finally, this book takes up where my previous book left off. While my book *How to Write a Thesis* (Murray 2002) concluded with a chapter on 'How to talk about writing', introducing the transition from writing to talking about research, this book covers all aspects of the viva. Important topics, such as recurring questions and strategies for answers, are covered in much more detail here.

Aims of this book

This book provides definitions, guidance and prompts for students, supervisors and examiners to prepare for the viva. The aims are to do the following:

- define the viva – the whole process;
- answer recurring student questions;
- unpack and explain 'grey areas';
- demystify the processes;
- define and illustrate the skills required by students and examiners for a successful viva;

- help students and examiners to prepare;
- help supervisors to prepare their students;
- help examiners to understand their role and develop their skills;
- explain question-and-answer processes;
- guide all participants in finding local information, making action plans and practising for the viva.

For students

Your viva is the moment when it becomes obvious, if it is not already obvious, that it is *your* project. Perhaps more importantly, it is your responsibility to find out exactly what will happen in *your* viva.

For everyone

The key point is to take account of research and good practice in your preparation, not just to listen to the myths, anecdotes and mystique surrounding the viva.

The main point

The viva is presented in this book as a new type of communication event. It is unlike any other event: not exactly an interview, not quite like other examinations.

Disaggregating

Disaggregating means breaking the whole – the thesis and the doctoral process – into its separate parts. The purpose is to find out: (1) exactly what went on in the research; (2) exactly what the thesis means; and (3) exactly what the student knows. While the thesis is a hermetically sealed argument, in the viva it is unpacked and reconfigured.

The discussion therefore includes the omissions, memories, gaps and discrepancies that are often 'smoothed' out of a submitted thesis. Since these topics will probably not have been the focus of as much discussion as those topics which did make it into the thesis, this could be a new set of talking points for students, and this can be a challenge.

Uncertainties

Such influential bodies as the Higher Education Funding Council for England set out practices and thresholds for the viva. Yet in all vivas uncertainties remain about: (1) which questions will be asked; and (2) the enduring and emerging questions about the research itself. However, this uncertainty need no longer shape the form and conduct of the viva. Nor should viva preparations be driven by uncertainty. Instead, it is the responsibility of participants to research local viva practice and to orient their preparations accordingly.

The style of this book

Readers will notice that I use a direct form of address to students. Since I take them to be the primary audience for this book, I address them as 'you'. However, from time to time the perspectives of examiners and supervisors are included. Supervisors and examiners who read drafts of this book did not find the style of address to be a problem and students liked it, so it has been retained.

Acknowledgements

Melanie Havelock has been the patient voice of Open University Press, and I want to continue to acknowledge the high level of professionalism at the Press at every stage in the publication process.

Participants at the Writers' Retreat, University of Limerick, in February 2002, listened to my early thoughts on this book. I want to thank them for their courteous and stimulating exchanges. For the Writers' Retreat itself I am deeply grateful, since I wrote my book proposal there. I want to thank Professor Sarah Moore, Dean of Teaching and Learning, for inviting me to be part of it.

Dr Vernon Trafford, at Anglia Polytechnic University, shared his research on the viva. Discussions and e-mail conversations with him informed my thinking about the viva, and I recommend his publications to readers of this book.

Dr Morag Thow is a constant source of inspiration, humour, enthusiasm and active distraction. It is difficult to say which has been most important. The humour . . . definitely.

Finally, although there have been many fruitful interactions with colleagues and students over the years, responsibility for every word of this book must, of course, reside with me. Where I have quoted students, I have done so anonymously because, while it is important to give them a voice, they do not always feel safe saying what they really think about the viva. I want to thank them for giving me permission to quote their words here.

1
Orientation

For most students, the viva is their first oral examination. For this reason, it is entirely appropriate to analyse it, to try to understand it from a number of angles and work out an informed orientation towards it. What is a viva?

> It is the physical contact with the examiners that makes oral examinations so unpopular with the students.
>
> (Gordon 1952: 165)

> It's a unique, exciting and fun opportunity to talk about your work
>
> (Anonymous experienced supervisor and examiner 2001)

> Nothing is more symbolic of the competitive climate in academe than the final oral in which committee members 'grill' candidates while they 'defend' their research. Committee members often compete among themselves, as if knowledge were combat sport, to see who can deliver the knockout blow.
>
> (Kerlin 1998: 16)

'Unpopular . . . fun?'

These three quotations capture the enigma that is the doctoral examination. On the one hand, it can be an extremely testing experience; on the other hand, it can be uniquely satisfying, since no one will ever listen as carefully to you talking about your work again. Because it is probing and, sometimes, competitive, it can feel like 'combat'.

'Physical contact' does not, of course, mean that you will be engaged in hand-to-hand combat; it means that someone will be physically present, in most circumstances, not only to ask you questions directly but also test your answers to those questions. Because they do this over an hour or two, they will be able to find out whether or not you *really* know your subject:

> Written answers have a certain remoteness about them, and mistakes and omissions, like those of life, can be made without the threat of immediate punishment ... But the viva is judgement day. A false answer, an inadequate account of oneself, and the god's brow threatens like an imminent thunderstorm.
>
> (Gordon 1952: 165)

All the quotations from Gordon (1952) are from the novel *Doctor in the House*, which, although it is a work of fiction, captures some of the tensions faced by candidates. 'Judgement day', for example, conveys the finality many students associate with the doctoral examination. The description of the examiner's facial expression conveys the student's sensitivity to the examiner's responses, both verbal and non-verbal. The doctoral examination is your one chance to impress examiners sufficiently to 'pass'. The fact that you will be judged on everything you say brings added pressure:

> If the candidate loses his nerve in front of this terrible displeasure he is finished: confusion breeds confusion and he will come to the end of his interrogation struggling like a cow in a bog.
>
> (Gordon 1952: 165–6)

There is also the knowledge that, normally, you go into the doctoral examination alone, with no one to support you. Even when supervisors are permitted to be present, they often have no speaking role. They may only be able to 'support' you silently.

Supervisors can feel under pressure too, since their supervision is, potentially, under scrutiny at this examination: if the student has made a terrible omission in the thesis, for example, is the supervisor at fault for not spotting it? Examiners, likewise, can feel under pressure, since so much rests on how they manage the whole examination process: for example, how much can they help students to do themselves justice, while still upholding the highest academic standards? It can be a difficult balancing act. Everyone in this examination, therefore, has reason to feel under pressure. This is why there is potential for so much tension in the room: even if one person relaxes, another may still feel tense.

In the minutes and seconds before the examination starts, you may wonder if it is all intended to make you doubt yourself. It certainly tests your self-assurance: 'I sat alone in the corner and fingered my tie. They always made the candidates arrive too early . . . There was nothing to do except wait patiently' (Gordon 1952: 168).

However, the doctoral examination need not remain an enigma. In fact, there is little sense in preparing for such an important event by simply resigning yourself to the fact that it will be an unpredictable interrogation. Besides, there is published research and documented practice to add to your collection of myths, hearsay and anecdote. It could be, therefore, that students are partly responsible for the mystique surrounding the viva. For too long they seem to have approached it with inadequate information. They have not taken a research orientation to their examinations: if something is so mysterious, we ought to research it. Chapter 2 begins the process with definitions and patterns of practice.

The doctoral examination requires a shift from a potentially passive, even 'victim', perspective to an active, even research, orientation. It may also require a change in orientation, from creating closure – in the thesis – to unpacking the research and writing processes – in the oral examination.

Research on the doctoral examination

While research on the doctoral examination is relatively new, there is an emerging set of studies of different aspects of policy and practice. This emerging body of knowledge can be characterized by researchers' focus on: (1) the candidate; (2) the institution; (3) the examiner; and (4) the phenomenon of information gaps.

1 *The candidate.* One group of researchers has focused on the candidate, on his or her performance and perceptions of this examination. This type of research draws on accounts of anticipated and/or reported experiences. There are very few observational studies that document what actually happens behind the closed doors of a viva. The themes of this body of research are mystique and mystification.
2 *The institution.* There is also some research on the institutions, their policies and practices. This type of research analyses and compares university documents and, in some instances, compares them with students' reported

experiences. The research shows variation in policy and practice between and within institutions.

3 *The examiner.* This type of research scrutinizes the text of examiners' reports. The finding is, again, that there is variation and evidence of inconsistency.

4 *Gaps in information.* Finally, there is a body of work focusing on the gaps in information that create the mystique surrounding the doctoral examination, including the lack of research and guidance available to examiners and students. There is ample evidence that doctoral students are uncertain about many aspects of the examination and some evidence that this creates high levels of anxiety and affects performance. There is also evidence, drawing on students' reports, of poor conduct by some examiners.

One of the first studies of the postgraduate experience, in the UK, was Rudd's *A New Look at Postgraduate Failure* (1985). Rudd conducted interviews with students and identified several problems that could be associated with non-completion. His findings suggest that 'failure' may start long before the examination. For example, students' poor writing strategies can create problems with their conceptual understanding and thesis production. In his chapter entitled 'What should be done?' Rudd provides a useful early warning:

> Many students already have regular supervisions at which they discuss written work with their supervisors. It was clear from my interviews that some of the others would resent this – this is another example of the gap that can develop between what the student wants and what he needs. Where, as will often be the case, the student's resentment flows from having achieved too little, and so having too little to report, the supervisor should not let the situation drag on to the inevitable failure, but should recommend that the student's registration be terminated.
>
> (Rudd 1985: 130)

The 'warning' here is, of course, for supervisors as well as students. In 1985, Rudd's proposed solution would have seemed radical, not only because there was much less in the way of routine, documented monitoring of student progress at that time but also because institutions were then, in general, much more reluctant to terminate a student's registration. However, nowadays there is likely to be much more readiness to take this course of action. This should mean that the student is unlikely to be judged an 'inevitable failure' at the examination stage, but there are always exceptions.

Delamont et al. (1997, 2000; Delamont 1998) have published important work on supervision and the doctoral experience. Like Rudd's, their research is interview based. One paper (Delamont 1998) reports that supervisors' practice is influenced by their own experiences as students, suggesting, to the strategic student, that it might be a good idea to find out a little about that, although some will no doubt find this a distraction. The main finding is that supervisors see their job as a 'number of balancing acts' (Delamont 1998: 163), in which they try to guide their students, while giving them enough freedom to develop independence.

If this is the case, then, for students, it emphasizes the need to communicate explicitly about what you need at the examination stage: explicit direction, practice or just general advice? It surely also implies the need for supervisors to prepare doctoral students for the examination, particularly since some students will not know exactly what they need. The trend that Delamont (1998) observes towards more systematic supervision suggests that supervisors should now be willing to provide examination guidance and preparation. Delamont et al.'s *Supervising the PhD* (1997) has a useful chapter – for students, supervisors and examiners – on preparing for the oral examination at this level. This book is aimed at supervisors, but the advice will be useful to students.

In the UK, there are several strands of doctoral examination research. Hartley (2000; Hartley and Jory 2000a, 2000b) catalogues the different forms of viva operating in different countries, while also considering students' views. Tinkler and Jackson (2000) have researched more thoroughly than anyone else the range of doctoral examination procedures and practices in UK universities. Trafford and Leshem (2000a) and Trafford et al. (2002) have done some of the most detailed work on recurring questions in the viva, based on observation of and participation in a number of examinations.

Wakeford (2002, 2009) has taken a case study approach to the role of the doctoral examination in supervision in his series of articles published in the *Education Guardian* over the past few years. He has amassed a collection of case studies, available at http://www.ucl.ac.uk/calt/phd-diaries/index.php#db, that provide evidence of bad practice in doctoral research supervision. He also reports cases where best practice has not been observed in the doctoral examination. His cases are an important body of evidence to draw on, based on student accounts of their experiences. This includes complementary evidence from supervisors and examiners. It is a tall order to provide such combined evidence for every institution, given the circumstances and ill feeling associated with such negative experiences, but until we have that, we have only part of the picture. Having said that, Wakeford's mini-narratives are convincing and do make a powerful case for more accountability in doctoral supervision and examination. For students preparing for the examinations, Wakeford's research could be useful in indicating lines of appeal if things go badly during the examination or if there have been problems with supervision.

Student responses to Wakeford's articles provide evidence of continuing problems, some of them quite acute (Wakeford 2002). In many of these quite serious cases, students have not been able to establish grounds for appeal, no matter how badly they were treated during the supervision process or during the examination.

While such practice-based insights are very important, and do teach us something about examination practices, the continuing lack of observational studies must limit the conclusions we can draw from this literature.

More recently, there have been attempts to articulate a doctoral curriculum, and to consider the role of the examination within that curriculum. This work has also considered the range of doctorates that are now operating and the range of examinations required for them (Boud and Lee, 2009).

Finally, while researchers have been diligent in their attempts to establish a theoretical and practical literature base on the doctoral examination, they have not accessed parallel, more developed literatures that could be adapted for this context. Consequently, we have not learned from research in other, related areas. For example, literatures on management practices, rhetoric and communications might be relevant, and some of the concepts from this literature have been adopted in other areas of higher education (Brennan et al. 1997). While it is arguable whether the concepts and techniques – and not just the terminology – of these new approaches have genuinely been adopted in practice, and while it is open to question that they sit well in their new context, these other literatures can open up new avenues for analysis and research of the doctoral examination.

For example, there are literatures on other forms of questioning that can inform our approach to oral examination for the doctorate. The techniques used in police interrogations, while not setting out to achieve the same purpose as the viva, do have similarities to the techniques that doctoral examiners are known to use. While this might seem an unusual parallel to draw, there are surprising resonances:

> Accepting negative feedback is thought to increase uncertainty, which increases susceptibility to suggestions. Accepting negative feedback is also likely to diminish an individual's self-esteem and increase anxiety, if only temporarily, making him or her more likely to attend to external cues rather than relying on his or her own internal frame of reference . . . making him or her more suggestible. The model does not assume that accepting negative feedback necessarily leads to an increased suggestible cognitive set, though it commonly does. For some, negative feedback may be construed as a challenge to improve, making them more critical of the situation and so less suggestible.
>
> (Bain and Baxter 2000: 124)

Again, this failure to access other disciplines that might have relevance for developing understanding of the doctoral examination, might have its origins in the myth that the viva is unique.

It seems sensible to acknowledge that there are questioning techniques that work to achieve particular ends and that it might be useful for students and examiners to know what they were. This would not only make examiners more aware of the forms of questions that have certain effects, but would also help students to prepare for their reactions to, for example, 'negative feedback', or to what appears to be negative feedback.

For example, there is at least one supervisor/examiner in the UK who says that he knows he only has to say the words, 'Oh . . . really?' to make a student question, or even begin to doubt, what he or she has said in a viva. This examiner says that if he then follows up that question with the question, 'Are you sure about that?', students are, often, perceptibly shaken in their thinking and are prompted to rethink the answers they have given in order to check them. The point here is not that examiners are unfair in asking such questions, but that they have usually built up an understanding of how to test students in the oral examination, and that students can be prepared for such questions. It is, after all, legitimate to ask the candidates to check their thinking, to ask them if they are 'sure' of what they have said and even to challenge their answers. Students are unlikely to have used the word 'sure' in their theses, and are likely to be wary of using it in their oral examinations. But, if they are asked, they have to answer. Students have to give clear, and clearly circum- scribed, accounts of what they are 'sure' about in their research. It is, therefore, an interesting question, but to an unprepared student it can sound like a criticism.

For the student, even implied 'negative feedback' requires a thorough answer, and this might mean that you have to be careful to ignore what this literature calls the implied negative external cue and continue to attend to your internal cues. Students who are not prepared for this type of question may fall prey to 'susceptibility', may lose their way in their answers or may contradict themselves.

While some readers will find the terminology used in the Bain and Baxter study alien or jargon-heavy, others will surely acknowledge that we risk being 'jargon-lite' in the viva literature. There is little enough definition to generate such a range of specialist terms. Others will see the quotation above as equivo- cal: the first interpretation gives way to a contradictory second one. Others will see that this is no more than the process of interpreting findings. The extract is, after all, taken from the midst of the paper. The purpose of the quotation is to illustrate the depth of research and analysis that is available in other fields.

What, therefore, can research teach us about the oral examination in the doctorate?

- Practice is variable between and within institutions.
- Certain questions recur across disciplines.
- There are disciplinary differences in the conduct of the doctoral examination.
- There are student reports of unfairness on the part of examiners.
- There is no set method for preparing for the doctoral examination.
- National and even discipline-specific guidelines on preparation for and conduct of the doctoral examination are not always followed.

The focus of viva research has been on the abstract politics of power relations, rather than on the specific rhetorical practices employed. This is the gap that this book sets out to fill.

Research orientation

One key point to take from this research summary is that there is a risk of generalizing from a small body of evidence. As long as the viva is a 'closed door' examination, there can be no evidence of good and bad practice. The student, therefore, has to become a researcher of local examination practice.

The research on the doctoral examination summarized above reveals a lack of clarity about the viva at institutional level. In viva workshops students reveal that they lack clear information about what will happen in their examinations. The same is true for supervisors and examiners: with few courses, only one or two textbooks, and an infinite variety of practices available on websites, many say that they deduce best practice from colleagues, codes of practice and anecdotes.

For students, as with other aspects of your work, a research orientation might involve a number of steps:

1   You can research the literature on the doctoral examination.
2   You can research actual examination practices at your institution.
3   You can shape your preparation for your examination according to the outcomes of such research.

The outcome of your viva research should be a clear set of aims and a programme for your practice sessions. This need not take a lot of time, but it does imply a systematic approach. Chapter 4 provides a timeline for the countdown to the examination.

You can – and should – calibrate your developing understanding of the doctoral examination with current practice at your institution. You will, of course, also have to calibrate your findings and thinking with your own style and personality.

Practice orientation

A research orientation is not, however, in itself sufficient. In this context, it is not adequate simply to develop your knowledge and understanding. You will also have to develop your practice. To some extent, you can even design your performance.

This means considering specific speech patterns, rhetorical strategies and behaviours that are going to be effective for you. It also means anticipating questions that are likely to come up (Chapter 5) and how you might answer them (Chapter 6). Above all, it means practising them. Entering into a sophisticated, sustained debate, which is what a viva is, requires you to take your existing skills to a higher level, well in advance of your examination.

This book draws on experiences of: (1) running viva workshops and one-to-one consultations with students preparing for the oral examination; (2) 'debriefing' discussions with students who have had their vivas; and (3) discussions with supervisors in a range of disciplines. In this sense, it has a practice orientation, and guides students in taking a practice orientation too, the focus of Chapter 8.

In Chapter 9 the subject of examination outcomes is addressed. Here too, however, there must be a reminder to students to research the practice at their own institutions, in order to be sure what the potential outcomes are for their vivas.

Finally, are research and practice discrete approaches? Does one not influence the other? How is best practice created? What influences its evolution? How can we evidence best practice without some form of research? While answering these questions may not be the examiner's, supervisor's or student's priority, it is important for all these participants to note that viva practice is evolving; it is no longer acceptable for a supervisor simply to assume that his or her doctoral student's examination will take roughly the same form as the previous one. Recent research and policy suggest that we have to be more systematic in our management of the doctoral examination. There is even talk of 'threshold standards' in research degree programmes, including the examination element of those programmes (Metcalfe et al. 2002).

Rhetorical orientation

This book is distinct from other writing on the subject, in that it prompts a rhetorical orientation to the doctoral examination. This means that all participants can approach this oral examination as a new type of communication event, requiring students particularly to review their analysis of audience and purpose, reconsider their modes of argument and upgrade their oral skills.

This rhetorical orientation makes sense of students' apparent confusion about so many issues before their vivas; this means that apparently basic questions about what this oral examination involves may be seen as entirely appropriate, as students 'start from scratch' to define the communicative context in which they have to work. Rather than treating such questions as naïve, therefore, perhaps we should see them as relatively sophisticated.

Positioning the doctoral examination as a new type of communication event begins to explain why new expectations are created and new skills are called for. It also repositions students about to take their vivas as – still – learners:

> There is . . . variation in how far students are prepared for the viva and how much they know about what is to happen or what to provide. In a survey of students in education who were close to completing their theses, 21 out of 84 were very uncertain about what criteria might be used by examiners . . . They believed that there are no objective criteria and that the outcome depends entirely upon the external examiner . . . However, other students had very actively asked staff about the form and content of their examinations, the specialisms of their examiners, and/or had attended sessions or mock vivas run by their departments.
>
> (Morley et al. 2002: 267)

As a student, rather than assuming that you are sufficiently 'expert' in the practices required for a doctoral examination, you may, quite rightly, feel that it is sensible to set out to learn about it before experiencing it. You might want to check some of the myths, assumptions and various sources of information available. If 'what to expect' and 'what will happen' are still topical questions in the research cited above, they are certainly legitimate topics for individual doctoral students to ask about their examinations.

Nor are direct answers to these questions sufficient; discussion and practice are crucial. Guidance will serve little purpose without practice. Repeat practice is more likely to lead to a reorientation of the viva event and an excellent performance by the student. In addition, advance discussion of a specific viva would be helpful to the internal examiner and supervisor, helping them, if they are new to this role, to develop their understanding and practice, and, if they are experienced, helping them to prepare.

Repositioning the doctoral examination as a new rhetorical event – for each student – potentially has the effect of making students' questions appropriate, even astute; it is smart not to assume that you know exactly what is expected, given the ambiguities surrounding the viva experience and evident in viva research. To dismiss students' questions would be to do a disservice to these intelligent people who have recognized that the viva is different from any other form of assessment that they have experienced. It is appropriate, therefore, for students to assume a position of little knowledge, but it is not appropriate to remain in that position until the examination. While viva research appears to show continuing confusions, we have to remember that lack of consensus may simply signal variations in practice. It does seem that, in this context, variation is the one constant.

Check your institution

Hartley (2000) reviews the various forms of oral examination used at the doctoral level across the world. The types of viva could be classified as follows. Where does your institution sit in this classification? How is the doctoral examination played out in your institution? Which format(s) is/are used at your institution?

Content	Examiners	Format
Thesis only?	Number?	Public?
Publications?	Roles?	Private?
Other work?	Supervisor?	Presentation?
Portfolio?	Assessors?	Set questions?
Performance?	Reporting?	Outcomes?
	Committee/Panel?	Duration?

Are these standards or variations? Research tells us that departments and institutions will vary, if they have any standard practice at all, and many do not.

Perhaps what is being tested in an oral examination is students' ability to reorientate themselves in this new communication event. The doctoral project is presented in a new way, shaped into a new form. The written thesis morphs into a set of spoken texts. The key transformation is that a single coherent text has to be rethought as a disaggregated set of questions and answers.

In addition, the student, who might have several successful academic performances under his or her belt, is now tested in the viva against a new 'gauge', to see if he or she can be brought into a new kind of alignment (with what?) or calibrated in a new way. Perhaps this is why the viva can feel like such an inquisition, or invasion: students' experiences suggest that they are being asked to 'fit' some new set of criteria, not of their own making.

Whether or not this is true or universal, it is important to acknowledge that a new communication event can bring disconcerting side-effects in the shape of questions of identity. What feels like a crisis of confidence may actually be a challenge to identity. For some, this will seem to be overstating the matter, but it is as well to confront the potential effects of this new event. Otherwise, in the worst case scenario, a student may balk at the requirement to present their work in a similar yet – yet again – different way. Some of the problems that occur in oral examinations may result from a mismatch of concepts or 'templates'.

Caffarella and Barnett (2000: 50) remind us of the need for doctoral students to learn to give and receive critiques. Although they were not focusing on the doctoral examination, some of what they say might apply here:

> Our recommendation . . . is that treatment of the scholarly writing process should include more in-depth material about both giving and receiving feedback. This might include guidelines as to what skills reviewers should possess, what types of feedback to include in the critiquing process, how to handle conflicting feedback from different professors, and an acknowledgement that being critiqued is both a rational and emotional process for most people, especially for novice scholars.

The giving and receiving of critiques orally might also require some training. The idea that the doctoral examination presents all participants – candidates, supervisors and examiners – with a new challenge is underscored by recent proposals that even external examiners would benefit from training (Metcalfe et al. 2002: Annex D).

Who should read this book?

This book is aimed at all students who are engaged in doctorates, including those just starting out and those who have a date set for their examinations. Those who are just starting may find that reading about the viva helps them to think more clearly about criteria. For those at the end of the doctoral process, the intention was to produce a short book making for, I hope, a quick read. The approach is to provide definitions, to raise questions that students need to find answers to locally and to prompt preparation and rehearsals.

Examiners will also find useful material here. There is, as yet, no other book that deals with the doctoral examination to this level of detail. In addition, there are implications in much of this material for how they play their roles. While they may not agree with everything that they read here, this book should prompt them to think through – and articulate – aspects of their role and their interactions with students before, during and after vivas.

Supervisors can use this book to help their students prepare for their doctoral examinations. Even if they do not agree with every single point, they can use this book as a starting point. For new supervisors, the summaries of scholarship and specifics of practice will be important. Experienced supervisors might complement this material with their knowledge and experience, as they mentor new supervisors.

Why do they need this book?

We know from the scant research, from many student reports and from hundreds of viva workshop discussions, that many matters and practices concerning the examination are not explained to doctoral students. Some students do not even know what questions to ask about their examinations. Some decide to wait and see what happens. Some are told that they do not need any special preparation: 'It's enough to know your stuff.'

It is therefore difficult to disagree with the assertion – though there are bound to be some who will – that students need to be better informed. They also need to be guided in the information they collect and what they do with it.

Even when information has been gathered, and even when it is acknowledged that practice is important, some students remain reticent about practising their skills. Because of this, this book offers numerous prompts to practise and guidance on how to rehearse.

What can go wrong

No matter how prepared you are, you cannot anticipate everything that will happen. However, you can be ready to think on your feet, to deal with the unexpected and to manage yourself, even if others are not managing their roles well:

> Probably the most disorganized defense I've attended is the one where the dissertation director began the meeting by saying, 'You've all read the dissertation. What questions do you have for the student?' What a mess. Questions started to be asked that bounced the student around from one part of the dissertation to another. There was no semblance of order and the meeting almost lost control due to its lack of organization.
>
> (Levine 2002: n.p.)

We have all heard horror stories about vivas, but how often do they actually occur? How do we know? Hardly any data are available on what actually happens in doctoral examinations. As we have already noted, everything happens 'behind closed doors'. Instead of being horrified at what you hear, however, you need to fill the information gap; they can't all go badly. This book is intended to guide your thinking about your examination, so that you can face up to the inevitable stressors and prepare to cope with them well.

Taken together, all of these points challenge the title of this book. Ultimately, the doctoral student's goal should not, in fact, be to 'survive' the viva; the goal is to do well, to do yourself justice, perhaps even to do very well in your viva. Whether or not you find it 'fun' – in anticipation or in reality – you can still prepare to give an excellent performance on the day.

Warning!

This warning message will reappear, in various forms, throughout this book, but it cannot be overstated. For a successful viva, you must do the following:

• Find out about doctoral examination processes and practices *in your institution*.

- Discuss the points raised in this book with your supervisor(s), colleagues and internal examiners.
- Contextualize the points in all of the chapters for *your subject and your thesis*.

While the general and specific guidance offered in this book is founded on published scholarship and established good practice, it is your responsibility to find more specific information, specific to your institution and, if need be, to your department and to the particular oral examination that you are going to participate in.

Checklist

- There is a growing body of research on the doctoral examination. Have you worked out what it has to say about your oral examination?
- Doctoral students can choose their orientation towards the oral examination: your options include research, practical and rhetorical orientations.
- Doctoral students, supervisors and examiners should check all the concepts and ideas presented in this book against their institution's regulations and procedures. Have you done a search for discipline-specific guidelines? See, for example, British Psychological Society (Psychology and related disciplines) (British Psychological Society 2000) and Mansfield (2008) (Chemistry). Is there a guide for your discipline?

2

What is a viva?

What is a viva – a doctoral examination? • Definitions • The role of the oral examination in the doctoral process • Mystique • Variation and variability • The concept of 'standard practice' • Codes of practice • Viva by videoconference • Individual or idiosyncratic? • Patterns in practice • Socratic dialogue • Criteria • Originality • Ambiguity • Disciplinary differences • Types of doctorate – types of examination • Personal preferences • 'Private graduation' • Not the end of the process • Checklist

Since it is clear that there are still some students who know very little about the viva, the next two chapters provide what might seem quite basic information. All the points covered are potential subjects of further, much more specific, discussion with supervisors well before the viva. For students at the start of their doctorates, these chapters can help you to shape your research and thesis, with criteria in mind.

This chapter covers many different definitions of the viva, or 'oral defence' or 'defense', in American English, in order not only to pin down but also to open up students' thinking about what the examination might involve. Common patterns of practice are defined, and students are encouraged to match their institution's practice to one pattern.

Given the apparently wide variation between and within disciplines, it is important to help students to realize that they have some 'research' to do on their institutions' and/or department's practices.

Check your institution

While this chapter performs the essential initial task in any argument of definition, prompting students to begin their preparations, the key point is that each student must check out and think through which definition, and which system, will be used in his or her institution, and in his or her examination.

What is a viva – a doctoral examination?

The viva can be seen not only as a defining moment in the doctoral experience but as, in many ways, *the* defining element of doctorate research. It is the final assessment of the research, the thesis and the student. Questions about, for example, how this examination is conducted, who will be there and how long it lasts have no definite answers. It is a new, high-level communication event, requiring advanced rhetorical and performance skills.

However, for some, the viva can be enjoyable:

> I enjoyed the viva so much because it was my opportunity to discuss my work with someone who really knew what I was doing and that was really important. I think that's what made it so enjoyable . . . it was more than me having to justify; it was more an exchange of ideas.
>
> (Student quoted in Murray 1998: 14)

But it can also be an anti-climax:

> I was examined by two very wise historians who didn't make the nitpicking queries which, while sitting in on vivas, I have heard people raise. It was like coming out of a doctor's surgery after being told that what looked like something nasty on the x-ray was only some coffee spilled on the film.
>
> (Sale 2001)

It can be discouraging, even when you pass:

> I sat the viva on my thesis. I came out a doctor, though it proved one of the most dismaying conversations I have ever had about my work. My examiners told me at the start that I'd got the PhD, but then used the rest of the viva to tell me how disappointing it was. The thesis was divided into two halves. They ignored the first half . . . and said there wasn't enough theory in the other . . . I felt they'd missed, or chosen to ignore, the point.
>
> (Shaw 1997: 21)

What would make examiners miss or choose to ignore this student's point? Does that say something about the examiner, or about the student? Is it because the examiner – and perhaps the student too – is following his or her own interests? Do they have preconceived notions about how you should answer their questions? More importantly, to what extent are examiners' expectations predictable? In other words, is it possible to prepare for this? Or is this student's comment no more than the result of their being tired and jaded? If you know your work so much better than anyone else, is it not likely that you will feel that you have not covered every one of the many – to you – key points in your thesis?

Bolker (1998: 128) writes about the viva moment as that point in time when you become aware of the gap between the thesis you thought you were going to write, at the start of the whole process, and the thesis you have actually produced. You are very aware of the flaws in your work and in your thesis. You can see its incompleteness. You may be unsure of the value of your work. You may be uncertain of its standard.

Normalizing these uncertainties is an important part of preparing for your examination. Accept that any piece of research you do will, in a sense, raise new questions and seem 'incomplete'. The doctoral examination is not, however, an occasion in which you try to fix all these perceived flaws: 'Examiners are impressed by thoughtful, reflective candidates who give consideration to constructive criticism and are able to modify their arguments accordingly' (Burnham 1994: 30). At the examination you can demonstrate that you have moved on and admit that you would do or write things differently now. This oral examination is, therefore, a retrospective discussion of a piece of work that is complete. In addition, since the thesis writer's thinking and other researchers' work continue, it takes in current, potential and future work.

Definitions

With so many variations in the viva, and so many unknowns, it is useful to start with definitions:

> The term 'viva' is an abbreviation of 'viva voce' meaning 'an oral examination' . . . The viva is a defence [of a thesis].
>
> (Baldacchino 1995: 74)

> The primary purpose of PhD assessment is to determine whether the candidate is competent as an independent researcher in the discipline.
>
> (UCoSDA 1993: 3)

The essential first step of defining terms is complicated further by the use of different terms for different aspects of the doctoral examination in different national and educational cultures, such as 'supervisor' or 'thesis adviser'. In addition, there is a steady supply of more complex – and various – definitions that appear to open up the doctoral examination to a wide range of practices:

> The [doctoral] examination is ... an opportunity to strike up a good working relationship on which you can later draw for references and in particular for recommendations when approaching academic publishers.
>
> (Burnham 1994: 31)

> When the thesis is sound and the external examiner is the right person, the 'examination' becomes something altogether more egalitarian and less confrontational than that term normally conveys.
>
> (Delamont et al. 1997: 148)

Check your institution

The definitions provided in these quotations are more complex, and perhaps more interesting for that. Some students prefer the simpler definitions with which this section started. Others find the complexity fascinating in theory, but terrifying in practice. Whatever your preference, it is important that you find out how those who will be involved in your examination, or your institution, define these terms.

The role of the oral examination in the doctoral process

If an oral examination is the defining moment of the doctoral process, an examiner's approach to it may depend on his or her initial assessment of the thesis:

> A number of academics suggested that the viva serves different purposes depending upon the quality of the candidate and her/his work ... In terms of the successful candidates ... the viva should provide them with experience and information ... For weaker candidates, the viva was often described as a forum within which examiners could provide constructive feedback and guidance ... For borderline candidates ... the viva allowed the candidate to 'defend' her/his work.
>
> (Jackson and Tinkler 2001: 360)

There is some evidence, therefore, that the viva is itself part of the assessment, although there is also evidence that a student's performance at the viva will not change an examiner's mind. This means that the oral examination still constitutes the final assessment and still requires an excellent performance from the student. It is, after all, compulsory.

The crucial – and perhaps initially alarming – inference here is that the oral examination may – or may not – decide the outcome of the examination of the thesis. At the time of writing it is well known – informally – that many doctoral examinations are decided on the strength of the examiner's reading, i.e. his or her assessment of the thesis before the candidate enters the room. Yet it is also well known that some oral examinations 'go to the wire'. The further implication here is that in the case of good or outstanding theses the oral examination matters less, though it cannot be said that this is always the case. Some examiners treat the oral examination more seriously than others. What we can say with certainty is that all candidates have to satisfy examiners that the thesis is their own work (i.e. not copied, plagiarized or written by someone else).

These differences are also reflected at institutional level:

> The balance between the assessment of the text and the viva or oral exam-ination is at least unclear and at best ambiguous. It is ill defined as to whether it is a one- or a two-stage assessment process, and what the rela-tive weight of the thesis is to the viva. For example, in some institutions, it is possible to fail the PhD on the basis of a satisfactory thesis but an unsatisfactory oral examination. In many, students can defend a some-what unsatisfactory thesis if they do a good viva.
>
> (Morley et al. 2002: 266)

Two types of institution are described here – which type are you in? What is its stand on this question? In order to establish the role of your oral examination, you would have to check local practice. In any case, whether your thesis is – or is considered – strong or weak, you should be ready to 'defend' it. In other words, you have a responsibility to make the oral examination the defining moment in your doctoral process by representing your work as of sufficient quality for the award. You cannot simply let your thesis 'speak for itself'; you have to find a way to talk about its strengths, while clearly demonstrating yours.

There is also evidence that the oral examination 'serves different purposes in different disciplines', although the researchers note that this finding requires further study (Jackson and Tinkler 2001: 361).

Yet the examination is not usually the driver of the research and writing in the way that other assessments often drive other forms of course or study. In fact, a doctoral research project is often completed and the thesis written without explicit reference to the criteria to be used in the examination.

This is not a reason to panic, nor is it a reason to rewrite your thesis, although you may feel – momentarily or regularly – like doing so. Instead, the role of the oral examination in your doctoral process is to make you focus on core questions, such as: did you do the work yourself?; can you talk about it convincingly?; can you see its strengths and weaknesses?; and have you become an expert in your field? This examination does require you to look back at your earlier work, and it is almost inevitable that you will see that as weaker in some way than your recent work. The key is to find ways to present your early (perhaps weaker) and your recent (probably stronger) research and writing in an integrated way.

Despite all these differences it is possible to generate a core set of principles about the purpose(s) of the doctoral examination that can then be used for more specific local discussions:

The oral examination: what it aims to find out

- Did you do the work yourself?
- Have you done the reading?
- Do you have a good knowledge of the field?
- Did you write the thesis yourself?
- Can you do research independently?
- Can you teach your subject?
- Can you talk about it professionally?
- Did you receive any training?
- Have you contributed to knowledge?
- Did you learn anything?

Doctoral examination practices will, of course, be shaped by individuals' and institutions' definition of the doctorate. In some areas – not all – the doctorate has evolved into a highly individualistic 'journey':

> Pursuit of the doctorate in most fields of study is a highly individualistic process. No two students' journeys are the same and nor should they be.
> (Kerlin 1998: 11)

> It is apparent that there is no single definition of the personal, intellectual quest on which doctoral students embark. Indeed we should not expect there to be one . . . Scientific and academic knowledge does not rest on a purely mechanistic set of definitions and requirements.
> (Delamont et al. 2000: 51)

However, given the current trend towards diversification in the doctorate, including five or six different types of programme (Hoddell et al. 2002) and perhaps as many types of thesis, there is clearly room for variation in examination practice. It makes sense that there is such variation.

In an ideal world, all of this would be the subject of extended and intriguing dialogue between students and supervisors: 'What *is* this "rite of passage?"', 'Who *are* the so-called gatekeepers?', 'What type of *career* is this leading to?', and so on. In practice, however, there is evidence that such conversations are sometimes rushed and, in some cases, left out of the preparation process altogether. Some would argue that these questions are completely irrelevant to your examination. Yet, for students, there will always be these 'big questions' underlying their concerns about the – possibly equally 'big' – questions that they can anticipate in their examinations.

For students who have good supervisors, the points covered in this chapter might be pretty obvious. For those who have poor, very busy or very laid-back supervisors, all of these sections will help students to determine what their oral examination will demand of them.

Mystique

> Surviving the viva depends fundamentally on preparation and students' ability to demystify the examination procedure.
>
> (Burnham 1994: 34)

At the time of writing, there has still been relatively little research on the doctoral examination. This has implications for the training of examiners: how do they learn to do their job? (Pearce 2005). In addition, until recently there were very sketchy guidelines – for supervisors or students – on what was likely to happen. This lack of information, along with the high stakes of the examination, have created a mystique surrounding the viva.

There are those who think this is how it should be. Because research is such a personal and individual experience, the examination should be private. This will be perceived as less true for those disciplines where research is conducted in much more 'public' ways. The most important point about any doctoral examination, after all, is not how everyone behaved on the day but whether or not you passed.

However, others view this oral examination's mystique as out-of-date, and even unfair. Voices in most UK institutions will tell you that they are aiming for more transparency. More and more universities now offer research training that usually includes discussion of the doctoral examination. All universities define the learning outcomes of their courses. Any assessment in higher education will have its criteria. Current thinking is that the mystique surrounding the doctoral examination is no longer justifiable on educational or perhaps even on ethical grounds.

As you gather information about the oral examination you may come across either view – you may meet people who do not want to 'tell you too much'. Some supervisors think that they will only frighten students by discussing the examination. Yet, in this way, these supervisors contribute to the mystique. Clearly, the sensible thing for the student to do is to press or negotiate for more definition and discussion. Expect a certain amount of mystique, 'grey areas', 'indefinables' and 'it depends' and be ready to persist with such questions as 'Yes, but how long is it *likely* to last?' and 'What is the *best* way to deal with questions about the weaknesses?' If need be, reassure your supervisor that you are not frightened by such discussions and let them see that you are not going to be fobbed off with reassuringly vague answers.

Variation and variability

What is clear from the research – and what is generally agreed among academics – is that there is variation in viva practice:

> What initially appears as common ground becomes less clear as the guidelines outlining practice . . . are examined more carefully. Indeed, setting aside considerations of seemingly 'common ground', our research reveals considerable diversity in policy regulating all aspects of the doctoral examination process.
>
> (Tinkler and Jackson 2000: 179)

The implications are that even if you do research doctoral examination practices at your institution, and do establish the range of variations currently operating there, you would be wise to expect further variability within that range. There may well be 'common ground' but there will be examiners who choose to take their own path. There is no map for this path: 'Where institutions do provide policy guidelines, there is . . . no common set of procedures for the organisation and conduct of the examination process' (Tinkler and Jackson 2000: 179). Research suggests that 'policy' does not always dictate 'conduct'.

What is confusing for students preparing for their examinations is the contradiction between the theoretical 'common ground' about examination practice and the lack of 'common . . . procedures' in practice. Just when you think you have worked out what is going to happen, you hear of another variation in practice. This can be frustrating, if you are looking for standard practice. At present, it might be more sensible to abandon the concept of standard practice, replace it with a core set of practices and prepare to cope if an examiner does anything outside that 'set'.

There are, finally, national differences. Hartley's (2000) short paper on 'Nineteen ways to have a viva' outlines the main types, including Australia, where an oral examination is generally not required.

The concept of 'standard practice'

While there is no such concept, in practice, there have been several attempts to establish a code of practice, or code of conduct, for the doctoral examination. Although there is evidence that use of these is patchy, it is perhaps worth discussing the appropriate code with supervisors in advance of your examination.

The British Psychological Society's (2000) guidelines are a good example, particularly Section 5.4, 'Conduct of the oral examination', in which the first point reminds examiners not only to make allowances for students' anxiety at the start of the oral examination, but to do something about it, i.e. in order to reduce it: 'The element of "ritual" should be acknowledged, but the candidate's understandable anxieties reduced to a reasonable level.'

Similarly, there are helpful suggestions for managing the end of the oral examination: 'Before the examiners disperse, there should be a debriefing discussion on the examination process. The Chair should take the lead, and encourage mutual assessment of roles.'

There are also specific guidelines on time: 'An oral examination should normally last for no less than one hour and no more than two hours.' While the word 'normally' is the usual academic code, leaving room for flexibility, this does begin to define the task.

Many students understandably expect more definite answers to their questions about the doctoral examination than are usually provided. However, the concept of standard practice is not universally established. It may not even be feasible to have standard practice in the context of research. Finally, even if that still seems absurd, it is no reason to let it get in the way of systematic preparation.

Codes of practice

First, and most importantly, there will be an internal code of practice, i.e. your university has one, and you should read it again now, having first checked that you have the current edition.

Second, there are external codes of practice, produced and distributed by quality assurance agencies or professional groups. For example, the UK has the Quality Assurance Agency's (QAA) *Code of Practice for the Assurance of Academic Quality and Standards in Higher Education: Postgraduate Research Programmes* (1999). The 'precepts' provide semi-specific guidelines. According to this code, institutions should inform doctoral students of assessment procedures, although neither the nature of those procedures nor the timing of the information is specified:

Institutions will wish to consider:

- the form in which postgraduate research assessment regulations and information should be made available to their research students, staff and external examiners, drawing attention to any exceptions or additional requirements that apply;
- the timing of the provision of such information;
- the mechanisms used for communicating procedures relating to the nomination of examiners, the examination process (including any oral examination), the process and time taken to reach a decision and the potential outcomes of the assessment.

(QAA 1999: 12)

That room for flexibility is being created here is apparent. However, this code does let students, supervisors and examiners know, if not exactly what information they have a right to expect, then the *types* of information that should be provided. (For a full discussion of all the precepts, see Eley and Murray 2009.)

Check your institution

Read your institution's regulations and procedures: 'assessment requirements and examination procedures' (QAA 1999: 5).

Perhaps the most useful point in the QAA code is the reminder that such information must be communicated to students, not at the end of their doctorates, just before the assessment, but right at the start, during induction. In fact, any sensible person considering undertaking a doctorate will probably have thought about assessment requirements at an even earlier stage. The question is whether or not the subject is addressed by the institution thoroughly.

There are also codes of conduct/practice issued by professional groups, such as the Royal Society of Chemistry, the British Psychological Society, which produced *Guidelines for Assessment of the PhD in Psychology and Related Disciplines* (2000), and others.

While it would be interesting to ask supervisors if they have seen or read these, in the meantime the growing importance of such documents has recently been pointed out: 'As higher education collides with the culture of accountability, and as the government pursues "quality assurance" throughout higher education, a reconsideration of the process of PhD examination is inevitable' (Wakeford 2002: 35). At present, however, there are more guidelines on the assessment of the thesis than there are on the oral examination.

A key question is the status of codes of practice. In general, they constitute less a contract between the student and the institution, and more an agenda for critical discussions between them. However, in time this too may change.

Finally, there is the additional question, prompted not only by such codes but also by institutional guidelines, as to whether simply presenting students with a written text is enough. Should there not be some in-depth discussion to ensure that students understand how guidelines translate into practices and for the context of their own doctorates?

Viva by videoconference

If circumstances prevent a face-to-face meeting, videoconferencing is an obvious and very good alternative.

(Pitt 1999: 28)

'After some initial strangeness' (p. 27), Pitt's experience of viva by video-conference was very positive. Lack of previous experience does not appear to have adversely affected this student, supervisor or examiner, and the paper allows us to learn from their experiences. Recommended steps would include a pre-viva meeting, to discuss procedures with technicians, agree seating and learn about the medium generally. Use of a visualizer helped the student to make his points clearly in diagrams.

In the case described, the external examiner was too ill to travel for the examination, but there may be other benefits to using this mechanism: for example, very busy, or previously unavailable, external examiners will save valuable time, and this mode might allow the supervisors and candidate to secure the services of their first choice. In addition, the cost of videoconferencing may be equivalent to the cost of travel, 'several hundred pounds' (Pitt 1999: 27).

While the effect of videoconferencing is often to formalize some aspects of communication, this will be seen by some as appropriate to the occasion of the doctoral examination. In some ways, the enforced turn-taking might prevent interruption of the student's answers, something that does occur in face-to-face oral examinations.

One barrier to overcome is the university's validation process; this mode of examination will have to be validated by the usual committees, and a protocol may be required. Some features of face-to-face oral examinations are likely to be retained, such as the need for the examiner's signature on the report form. Those concerned not to reinvent the wheel can start with Appendix C to Pitt's paper, which reproduces Edinburgh University's 'Guidance notes/checklist for oral examinations by video link' (Pitt 1999: 44).

Key safeguards in the Edinburgh guidelines include the requirement for training for candidates and examiners, the presence of those with technical expertise at both sites and the stipulation that the candidate has to give written agreement to this form of examination.

Check your institution

Everyone involved will have to check the characteristics of both: (1) video-conferencing, specific to their local contexts; and (2) the protocol for conducting a doctoral examination in this way at their institutions.

Check, carefully, that you understand and agree on your interpretations of protocols and procedures.

Other aspects of using videoconferencing for teaching and learning are also covered in this publication. This is, for many, a relatively new procedure, and policies and protocols are still being developed in some places. However, some institutions have a body of experience that students, supervisors and examiners can consult. Students should ensure that they receive copies of relevant protocols in good time. While it might seem unfair to land this responsibility on students, given that it should surely lie with institutions, the purpose of this book is to flag up how students can take an active role in gathering the information they need.

Given the novelty and potential for added stress, you may – or may not – have the right to refuse to be examined in this medium, particularly if you have reservations about the management of the process or the lack of training or protocol for supervisor and examiners, or if your questions have not been answered. It may be that supervisors and examiners themselves will have similar reservations. You can at least check whether there will be any briefing and/or training in this medium.

Individual or idiosyncratic?

In this context the word 'individual' suggests that every doctoral examination is different. Each has, potentially, its own criteria and set of practices. 'Idiosyncratic' suggests that the individuality of a doctoral examination is particular to one person, be that the supervisor, the student or the examiner. In reality, in the UK, at the time of writing, it can safely be assumed that it is the examiner or independent chair who will have most influence on the conduct of the oral examination.

While each doctoral examination has elements that are particular to the study conducted, and to the thesis written, it is not true to say that each is completely different from every other. While any doctoral examination will seem idiosyncratic to someone, there are core practices. There is a set of core criteria. At any one institution, there ought to be a written code of practice and a record of what took place at each examination. Not that this will necessarily be widely distributed, read and discussed. Perhaps that is the problem: in the absence of any comparative information, we are left to reinvent the doctoral examination each time it occurs.

The point of this short discussion is to begin the argument that aiming for individuality can lead to idiosyncrasy. There should be some level of 'common ground' in all doctoral examinations in your discipline, your department or your institution.

There must be some level of consistency of practice within a department and/or discipline. 'Every doctoral examination is different' should not, therefore, be the last word in our attempts to define this form of examination for ourselves; instead, it is a starting point. There should be some degree of synchronicity – not necessarily uniformity – across all doctoral examinations. In other words, your examination will be different from others in some respects, but similar, perhaps even identical, in others.

Patterns in practice

In the midst of the documented diversity of doctoral examination practice, you will see patterns:

Format

- *Discussion.* The oral examination is an extended debate.
- *Presentation, discussion.* The examination begins with the candidate's presentation, followed by discussion.
- *Working session.* The examination includes demonstration by the student of skills/analyses.

Roles

- Supervisor takes notes.
- Supervisor is silent.
- Supervisor offers support.

Outcomes

- Decision announced at start.
- Decision announced at end.
- Decision announced when candidate returns from brief spell outside examination room.

Once you know which pattern is likely to occur, you can practise in that way.

However, you have to be ready to cope with the examiner who breaks the pattern, who, for example, asks you a question in the midst of your presentation. What do you do? Raise the point explicitly: remind him or her that you all agreed that you would give a presentation first and take questions second? Point out that you are going to cover the point of his or her question in your presentation and ask if you can continue with your presentation? There may be no sinister reason for the question; the examiner may simply, genuinely, be interested in what you are saying. The point of this example, however, is that students should also prepare to cope with deviations from agreed examination formats.

Socratic dialogue

Occasionally, the doctoral examination is referred to as a form of Socratic dialogue, suggesting that the questions asked serve the purpose not only of testing the candidate's knowledge, but also of advancing it:

> Socrates believed that he had a duty . . . to teach through questioning people's beliefs . . . His famous 'Socratic irony' (pretence of ignorance) and his 'Socratic method' of skillfully directing his questions to obtain the answers he wanted could appear at first sight to produce only negative results; those he questioned were shown that their assumptions were ill-founded. But this was a necessary preliminary to the start of serious discussion with defined terms.
>
> (Radice 1971: 222–3)

There are some examiners who will want to use the doctoral examination to 'teach' you something, not in the traditional sense – though what does and does not constitute 'teaching' is open to debate – but in a more subtle way. Genuine experts in your field will want to try to draw you out, to see if you understand the implications of your work as well as they do, or in the way that they do. They will be genuinely intrigued to see where you can and cannot take your ideas. They will be interested to see how you articulate your ideas in a dialogue with them. They may even see it as a bit of a challenge, a chance for them to sharpen their own debating skills. Some will be motivated to help you develop your thinking, and may be less concerned with how you express yourself. The truly skilled examiner will find a way to open your mind to new possibilities, to see the limitations of your work in a positive way and to recover your excitement for research.

This is not to say that you should be manoeuvred out of making a strong case for your own assumptions and beliefs. Instead, you should, of course, continue to make a strong case for the work you have done and the text you have written, but you might also consider yourself free to follow the examiner's line of thought, if you find it interesting. Just to keep things clear, you might say, at some point, that that is what you are doing.

Criteria

There are no universal, precise or explicit criteria for a successful PhD.
(Wakeford 2002: 35)

Not all staff seemed to be aware of the indeterminate criteria ... the criteria for success and failure in the PhD cannot be reduced to a set of written rules.
(Delamont et al. 2000: 40)

Criteria for the doctorate are difficult to pin down. Some are contradictory. For example, candidates are asked to make a claim for 'originality', while also showing 'intellectual modesty' (Delamont et al. 2000: 40), an almost impossible balance to strike. Too much of one will quickly overshadow the other.

While criteria for examining the doctoral thesis are available, if complex, it is more difficult to find criteria for the oral examination. Which criteria will be used to judge your performance?

Burnham (1994: 32) states that the 'most common criteria' are:

1 Has the candidate clearly laid out the problem to be addressed?
2 Has the candidate 'consistently developed this theme throughout the chapters'?
3 Has the candidate 'skillfully stated the relevance of the conclusion for the discipline'?

However, these too seem to be about the thesis rather than the oral examination. Similarly, the British Psychological Society (2000: 12) has extremely helpful guidance on 'Criteria to be used in assessing the written submission'. Are we to presume that these are also used in oral examinations, or not? Or are there other criteria to be applied to the oral examination, and, if so, would these relate more to the candidate's performance?

'Of publishable standard' recurs across sets of criteria for the thesis. You should have some view of which parts of your thesis are – and are not – publishable. In which journals are you most likely to publish this work? This is a demonstration of your knowledge of the field. Talking about your work in these terms is the task in the doctoral examination.

Mullins and Kiley (2002: 378–9) have defined the qualities of poor and outstanding theses, based on interviews with experienced examiners, as follows. Characteristics of a poor thesis were:

- lack of coherence;
- lack of understanding of the theory;
- lack of confidence;
- researching the wrong problem;
- mixed or confused theoretical and methodological perspectives;
- work that is not original;
- not being able to explain at the end of the thesis what had actually been argued in the thesis.

Terms used, in the same study, to describe a good thesis included 'scholarship', 'originality', 'coherence', 'sense of student autonomy or independence', with a well-structured argument being valued in terms of 'conceptualisation, conclusion, design, logic and structure' (Mullins and Kiley 2002: 379).

As indicated earlier, there is some debate about whether what is being assessed in the doctoral examination is the thesis, the student, or both. Research suggests that this may depend on the discipline, or on the strengths/ weaknesses of the thesis or on the individual examiner's practice and/or standing in the field. It is probably safe to assume that both thesis and student are subject to assessment on the day. However, the criteria for assessing a thesis, reviewed in this section, can be translated into performance criteria, specific discursive acts and issues for debate in the oral element of the examination. Many of the criteria are clearly open to debate. That is entirely the point of the examination: to prompt the student to debate the value of his or her work.

Whatever the examiner's stance, and whatever the criteria used, there is one positive note – and a useful reminder to keep things in perspective – in Mullins and Kiley (2002: 384): 'For students, the most heartening information is that experienced examiners want them to be awarded the PhD and will go to extraordinary lengths to enable this to happen.' Experienced examiners are aware that several years' work is assimilated in a thesis and that revisions and further work have a cost to the student and to the institution. They may be more likely to be 'tolerant' than 'forensic' in their assessments of theses (Mullins and Kiley 2002: 384).

Originality

Phillips and Pugh (2000: 63–4) provide a wide range of definitions of 'originality'. In any discussions with students, supervisors or examiners, the range would be equally wide. Yet there is general agreement that this remains the key criterion of doctoral research for many individuals and institutions. The word even appears on examiners' report forms.

Examiners are aware that originality can be defined in a number of ways, and they will look for this quality in your thesis:

> I'm quite nervous about examining this PhD . . . Looking for originality and excitement, critically. A PhD has to have something about it that's theoretically exciting, and original, without being world-shattering . . . But I think originality is the critical thing. And excitement. Something that grabs you. It's not just a competent pragmatic piece of work. There's something behind it that shows the person is engaged in the debate.
> (Delamont et al. 2000: 36)

Whether or not you have used the word 'originality' in your thesis, you should be prepared to use it in your responses at your oral examination, so that you can show: (1) that you understand what is – and is not – original in your field; and (2) that you can judge the degree and type of originality in your own work within that field. In fact, it could be argued that the word should be in everyone's thesis abstract and conclusions.

If you do not feel comfortable using the word 'originality' in relation to your research and thesis, then you must either find a way to become comfortable with it, by clarifying its relevance to your research, or use some other word with a similar meaning, such as 'new', 'different', 'fresh' or even 'alternative to traditional'. Whatever word you choose, use it in your practice sessions. It might help, not only in terms of developing your confidence in talking about your work in this way but also in terms of clarifying the type of 'contribution' you can claim, to define and delimit your specific contribution: i.e. 'contribution in the sense that [define] . . . and to the extent that [delimit] . . .'.

Ambiguity

This is another concept that recurs in discussions of the doctoral examination and its form and function. There may even be supervisors and examiners who see their role almost as custodians of ambiguity, with the candidate playing the role of a kind of apprentice 'ambiguity worker'. Many examiners see one of their roles as identifying ambiguities and contradictions in the thesis and then teasing them out with the student in order to establish: (1) that the student sees them; and (2) that the student can revise his or her views and/or statements, sometimes there and then, appropriately.

In addition, since this oral examination is in many ways a transition point for the developing researcher, there are ambiguities embedded in doctoral examination interactions:

On the day a robust performance is required but be careful to avoid dogmatism.

(Burnham 1994: 30)

An original contribution to knowledge, a nebulous phrase which constitutes a potential ambiguity.

(Baldacchino 1995: 72)

The student is urged to be independent in scholarly endeavor. Training an individual to be independent in an authoritarian social structure has a potential paradoxical quality, that is not always recognized by the agent. In effect, professors say to students, 'Become an independent thinker; be critical, innovate, and question the established body of knowledge; but remember, we will be the sole arbiters of what you must do and how well you go about it.'

(Gardner 2008: 326)

Should we take these statements to mean that even the key criterion could be ambiguous, or, instead, should we take them to mean that the terms 'robust', 'original contribution' and 'independent' are open to interpretation?

There are other potential ambiguities in the doctoral examination:

- the oral examination should be transparent/it should retain its mystique;
- the oral examination is a formal examination/the criteria are 'indeterminate' (Delamont et al. 2000: 40);
- the thesis is examined/the examiner can ask about anything;
- the student is an expert/the student is a novice;
- 'the examiner is not out to get you'/we have all heard horror stories;
- standards and practices are defined/no one can predict what examiners will ask or how they will ask it.

The trick is not to be thrown by such apparent contradictions but to find your own way through them.

Disciplinary differences

Differences between – and within – the disciplines of academic study are bound to have consequences for the doctoral examination cultures in each area:

In sociology, the responsibility for deciding on the precise research problem and methodology would be the student's. In science, the problem and method are determined by the supervisor in advance. A thesis in economics can comprise three publishable articles. In philosophy, a coherent examination of a single question would be required.

(Wakeford 2002: 35)

This is quite a wide range of differences, each with implications for the doctoral examination. As the day of the examination draws near, the student is likely to be well aware of the type of doctorate he or she has completed and the type of examination that he or she can expect.

Many academics – i.e. those experts in their area of study, not researchers on the doctoral examination – would argue in the strongest terms that the doctorate and the examination take quite specific forms in their disciplines, and that these forms are completely different from those in other disciplines. This may be one of the reasons for students' anxieties: that the people who hold most power in their area argue for consistency in their area, while many students are only too well aware of diversity in practice.

If your supervisor is adamant that there is only one type of doctoral examination in your discipline, then you have at least to appear to take on board what they say, for obvious reasons. However, this does not mean that you cannot – or are not 'allowed' to – do some research on doctoral examination practices yourself. It would be pointless to try to argue this case with your supervisor; it would be equally pointless to prepare only for the type of examination he or she anticipates, without checking, unless you are sure that your supervisor has done the homework on the doctoral examination at your institution. You may be able to judge by his or her answers to your questions about your examination.

Types of doctorate – types of examination

While it has been argued that the alternative form of doctorate 'meets the same demands of the traditional PhD' (Allpress and Barnacle 2009: 165), there may be significant differences. Different types of doctorate have different requirements of the thesis: for example, some doctorates may include course work, and some theses may be shorter. The impact of these differences on the examination is – like other aspects of the doctoral examination – by no means standard, either across the higher education sector or across national higher education cultures. This suggests that the types of researching and checking recommended in this book for so-called 'traditional' doctorates are also appropriate for other doctorates, such as professional (Scott et al. 2004), work-based, practice-based (Winter et al. 2000) or project-based doctorates (Allpress and Barnacle 2009). In other words, some aspects of these different types of doctorate may raise similar questions.

On the other hand, it may be that the differences between these doctorates and the PhD have not been fully explored, in terms of their content and learning outcomes, and that consequently the forms of assessment for these different doctorates have not been fully developed: 'there is a tension in the assessment methods employed by DBAs [Doctor of Business Administration] through their relationship with the traditional PhD' (Ruggeri-Stevens et al. 2001: 61). Ruggeri-Stevens et al., having surveyed a selection of DBA programmes in the UK, demonstrate the range in practices, including, in some cases, an oral examination as part of the assessment process, do not have findings specific to that element of DBAs, but they do raise questions about external examiners:

> Are external examiners, who are presumably used to assessing PhD theses, properly prepared to assess dissertations with a wider range of success criteria or do they simply apply the PhD criteria with which they are familiar?
>
> (Ruggeri-Stevens et al. 2001: 70)

This potential problem is also raised by Evans and Kamler (2002): 'there is likely to be a large volume of work to be examined by people who are unfamiliar with the types and purposes of the texts before them' (p. 105). While they raise this issue in relation to examination of written work, it may also have relevance for the oral examination.

Much of the distinction between the PhD and other types of doctorate hangs, course, on differences in the definitions of the work and research: 'The role of written to practical work within practice-led research does not fall neatly into two categories: information versus data, for example' (Swift and Douglas 1997: 20). By the time they come to the examination, most if not all students will be aware of most if not all of these differences, but they may want to think through their implications for their examination.

With no data base, it is impossible to provide a definitive resolution to this issue, but doctoral students should not only ensure that they themselves are aware of the criteria to be used in their examinations but can also check that their supervisors ascertain that external examiners know what they are. These criteria will then shape practice sessions, although some will argue that students should also practice coping with examiners who go 'off message', i.e. who seem to use different criteria. The point is not that students should be ready and willing to answer questions derived from any criteria the examiner chooses to use, but that students should develop coping strategies for this type of challenge.

Alternatively, there may be a more flexible approach to professional doctorates: 'Professional or research-coursework doctorates are seen as being more flexible than research-only PhDs, and they attract a wider variety of candidates with varying interests and work backgrounds when compared to PhD candidates' (Sarros et al. 2005: 155). Sarros et al.'s study was located in the Australian higher education system, where there is no oral examination for the doctorate, but some of the issues they raise about procedures and protocols are relevant to students, supervisors and examiners preparing for the viva.

However, there may be quite well-defined differences between the PhD and doctorates in disciplines like art and design, where it is not just a written text that is being examined:

> The viva therefore takes on a more significant role than just the opportunity to ensure the identity of the researcher. It may be the first real opportunity for the researcher to demonstrate fully the connections between practice and research, the effect of research on practice, and the embodiment of research within practice. These may only be alluded to or outlined through the juxtaposition of image and text within a classical document but not demonstrated as fully as is possible in the presence of the work.
>
> (Swift and Douglas 1997: 21)

Swift and Douglas go on to raise questions about whether, if this is the process that institutions require students to progress through, it should be left till the examination stage, or whether the exhibition should occur before the examination, i.e. should the exhibition be part of the research process, or should it be part of the examination? Their guidance is specific to their discipline, but many of the points they raise are relevant to other disciplines, and their guidance is in line with the more detailed guidance offered in this book.

In other disciplines, such as architecture, the nature of the question-and-answer part of the oral examination may have a different purpose, and examiners may have different roles:

> Candidates in the RMIT [Royal Melbourne Institute of Technology] School of Architecture and Design mount a public exhibition of their work. They are examined through a presentation and defence of the thesis in front of a panel of three examiners . . . they ask clarifying questions that seek to elicit further exposition of the research from the candidate. Final assessment takes into account the candidates' exhibition, their verbal defence of the work and their framing exegesis.
>
> (Allpress and Barnacle 2009: 164)

In this context, as in others described in this book, there is room for interpretation of components and criteria. For example, students would wish to know whether or not all the elements of this assessment have equal weight. They might want to know whether any specific weighting was recommended in the institution's regulations, code of practice, procedures or guidelines for examiners and students, to discuss how this weighting had been applied in recent examinations and to be reassured that this weighting would be applied to their assessments.

Finally, this is not to say that examination of the PhD will not include any of the above issues, since in some areas the professional or practical applications of the student's research are appropriate subjects for examiners' questions and discussion.

Personal preferences

Once you have defined the nature of the viva in your institution, you may find that there are variations in practice. If different vivas can be conducted in different ways, you may realize that you have preferences among these variations. For example, you may prefer to have your viva in the morning, if you find that you are fresher or more comfortable working then. Or, if you do your best thinking in the afternoon, you might want to press for a later time. Or you may prefer to give a presentation at the start, giving you a chance to have your say and represent your work as a whole, or you might prefer to go straight to question-and-answer.

You may not be offered any such options, but you can ask and, if need be, and if you feel it is appropriate, negotiate with your supervisor and examiners. Remember to tell them what you want explicitly. This does not, of course, guarantee that they will grant you what you wish, but it does at least mean that they will know what you want. If you do not tell them, they cannot know. Simply dropping hints is not enough. Besides, time may be short and listening skills – theirs and yours – may be tuned to a lower frequency than you are used to.

'Private graduation'

When you defend your thesis it will become much clearer to you that you own this work, that such ultimate decisions are yours, and, what's more, that you most likely know more about your subject than anyone else does … This realization is an important *private* graduation, a psychological parallel to the public ceremony.

(Bolker 1998: 134)

What are the pros and cons of looking at the doctoral examination this way? On the one hand, it prompts you to make the transition to being a peer, once you have had your internal graduation moment, but on the other hand you still have to behave as if it is an examination, because it is. Of course, it is important that you feel some sense of security in your work. If you are to perform at your best, you have to develop a sense that what you have done is, at least in part, your best work.

Why is it 'private'? Clearly, it will do you no good at all if, in your oral examination, you act as if you have already graduated. The valuable point that Bolker makes is that there is an important psychological turning point, which each student will potentially make at a different stage. Some will realize early on that they have made a significant contribution; for others, more effort will need to go into active construction of the 'contribution' the thesis has made. For students to perform well in the oral examination, it is important that this work is done before – not during – the examination.

Not the end of the process

The oral examination is built up to be 'the end' of the doctoral process, but in reality the doctorate does not end there. There is almost always more work to do. As will be discussed later, you will probably have more work and/or writing to do after your examination. Since the most common outcome is a pass with revisions and/or corrections, then you are not quite finished. Nor is it the end of the world if you have to do some more work; most people do. Do not, therefore, let the stakes get too high, so that it will seem like the end of the world if you have more work to do.

What the doctoral examination is, is an initiation into peer review. It is at once similar to and different from the type of peer review we receive on journal articles and research or book proposals. The main differences are that it is conducted not at a distance, over time and by anonymous reviewers, but face-to-face and in real time. The doctoral examination is not, therefore, the end of this type of scrutiny of your work. Peer review continues throughout academic, research and other careers, perhaps in different forms.

Checklist

- There is a mystique and ambiguity surrounding the doctoral examination – use your institution's regulations and code of practice to work out what's going to happen at your examination.
- Find a way of talking about your 'contribution' in a way that suits you and your research.
- This is an examination. Focus on criteria – work out what else you have to do.

3

Roles and responsibilities

Anecdotes • Approaches • Rhetorical design: audience and purpose •
Examiners • The panel • Roles • The independent chair • Questions to ask
at your institution • Audit your existing skills • Checklist

Anecdotes

Every institution, every supervisor and every examiner has his or her supply of
anecdotes. These are not, however, the best sources of information about what
is likely to happen at your oral examination. Be wary of predicating your
assumptions on and shaping your practice according to this unreliable source.

Approaches

As you approach your examination, you might find yourself corresponding to
one of the following categories of candidate.

The ostrich

I'd rather not think about it now.

You stick your head in the sand. You put off thinking about the examination.
You decide that since it is so obscure there is no way you can prepare anyway.

The big question here is how long you let 'now' go on for. In the first year this might be a wholly sensible approach. In the third year, particularly towards the end of that year, it becomes less sensible.

Them-and-us

They're out to get me.

You see the examiners as adversaries and assume that they will see you that way too. You see the examination as no more than the enactment of the conflict between those who know – and hold power – and those who do not. There is a grain of truth in this position: the examiners are out to probe your thesis and test your knowledge, perhaps to its limits. They may well be out to find out where those limits lie. This attitude towards the doctoral examination may be fuelled by hearsay and anecdote.

Examination

What do I have to do to pass?

If the viva is an examination, there must be a set of criteria. There must be limits to what the examiners can ask you. You position yourself as a student who has to prepare for a specific task. This too is sensible. However, there is an element of surprise in the oral examination. You cannot predict which questions will come up; nor can you predict exactly how the examiner will assess your answers. For successful exam passers – and doctoral students must have been good at exams to get to this point – this is a new type of examination.

Discussion

I know what they'll want to talk about.

This approach assumes that candidate and examiner are more or less on equal terms. They share a common interest or area of expertise. Although it is true that the doctoral examination does revolve around discussion, there is a risk that some candidates with this attitude interpret the examination as a 'cosy chat'. Occasionally it is, but usually it is not.

Ordeal

I don't know anything.

You are simply terrified at the prospect of the oral examination. More candidates experience fear and acute anxiety before their examinations than you might imagine. So, if you are thinking this way, you are not alone. Not that it should be an ordeal, of course, but there are elements of the ordeal about it: the stakes are as high as they possibly could be, the examiner is an expert in your field and, despite your best attempts at researching the examination, there are still many unknowns. You may also be expecting nothing but a barrage of criticism of your work, when, in fact, all you have to do is show that you can take criticism and critique it yourself.

Formality

Is that it?

If the doctoral examination seems like a formality to you, you will feel that you have already passed. Again, it is easy to see where this attitude comes from, particularly if your work is excellent. In order for you to progress to the oral examination, your thesis must be deemed by your supervisor to be worthy of submission:

Nowadays . . . by the time you get to your defense, the assumption is that you will pass it and finish your degree. Most graduate programs are much more careful than they used to be about monitoring the progress of their students and screening out early those whom they don't think will be able to make it.

(Bolker 1998: 133)

This suggests that you have already met the required standard. That is, of course, not entirely true; you still have to be examined. So it is not in any sense a formality. If, in the run-up to or during your examination, you act as if you assume that you have passed, you may find that an examiner sets to work to correct that assumption. This may be the origin of some of the aggression that sometimes bubbles up in doctoral examinations: the examiner feels the need to correct the misconception that the student has already passed and asks harder questions, takes a harder line in questioning and puts a harder edge on the discussion. In this scenario it is as if the examiners feel that they have to reconstruct the experience of an examination for such students, in order to make them realize that writing a good thesis, and even getting excellent research results, are not in itself sufficient.

In other words, while Bolker (1998: 133) has made a useful point about the shifting role and status of the doctoral student at the time of the examination – 'act like a professional and an expert in your field, as part of proving . . . that you are ready to make the shift' – we should be clear that what she advocates is performance of 'readiness' to become a peer of the examiner. The doctoral examination puts down a marker that you are not quite there yet. It asks you to acknowledge that parts of your thesis represent the immature phase of your work and your developing understanding. This is not to say that you should simply concede that, yes, your work could always be improved, but that you should make the case for specific changes that would improve the research and against others that you think would not.

To complicate matters further, we all know of cases where candidates have been told that they have passed the examination as soon as they enter the room, i.e. right at the start of the examination. While many may see this as an ideal opportunity to relax, in fact you still have all the work to do. Everything in the previous paragraph still applies. In reality, you might find this even more demanding. Some students report that they have been so 'psyched up' for their oral examinations that when they were told in the first minute that they had passed, they felt completely deflated, even overwhelmed. It can be a confusing moment, since, it is worth repeating, you still have it all to do.

The extent to which any of this happens is, of course, open to debate. In the absence of good local or national data, we have no way of knowing. What we do have, however, is a set of experiences – of students, examiners and supervisors – that we can analyse and use to understand the doctoral examination.

Perhaps the best approach is to take a critical stance on your own work, and after several years of work, this is usually not difficult. The shift required is from constructing a narrative and sound argument for the interpretation of your research and the contribution you have made, on the one hand, to a kind of interrogative flexibility, on the other. Instead of performing a reporting function, as we do in writing a thesis, we perform a reflexive function. Your thesis, which has, as a text, stood apart from other texts, now goes public and joins the debate. In a sense, it might help if you can see it in a different way, while still seeing it in the old way. This might require changes in the cognitive, behavioural and affective domains.

Rhetorical design: audience and purpose

The essence of a rhetorical approach to the doctoral examination is to see it as a new type of communication event. In some ways, it is likely to be different from other discussions of your research and writing. It is entirely appropriate, therefore, not only to consider audience and purpose, but to analyse them, rethink them thoroughly and design your behaviours in this new context. Treat it as a new event and prepare to make some changes in your assumptions, your expectations and your behaviours. Even familiar faces may be called upon to play new roles in the doctoral examination as internal examiners, for example. Each of these roles may have quite specific local definitions, while it is unlikely that all of the following will participate in every doctoral examination.

- *Supervisor/thesis advisor/tutor.* Refers to the member of academic staff who works closely with the student over the full term of the doctorate.
- *External examiner (1).* Designates a member of academic staff at another institution who is the chief examiner.
- *External examiner (2).* In some countries the external examiner is from another department, but is not always the chief examiner. For inter-disciplinary research this might be a second member of staff who is competent to examine in a second area.
- *Internal examiner.* Designates a member of academic staff in the candidate's department or faculty, often, but not always, knowledgeable or with some expertise in the area of student's research or in a related area; may also conduct progress reviews during the doctorate.
- *Chair.* Refers to the external examiner or neutral academic, depending on the country/educational system. The neutral academic may have had no previous contact with the research and thesis being examined. In some countries the supervisor chairs the examination; in others, supervisors may be present but play no active role.
- *Committee.* The group of academics involved in the project, including the supervisor, external and internal examiners and perhaps others.
- *Independent chair.* Responsible for conducting the examination in a way that ensures that the regulations and procedures of the institution are followed.

Each of these terms might have slightly different meanings in practice in different institutions in the UK or in the USA. Moreover, when there are so many experts in one room, there is the inevitable fraught question of their relative status. If there are two examiners it is probably important for the student to know their relative status. It is also important for candidates to realize that it is by no means standard practice to have supervisors or chairs present. However, the increasing use of the independent chair goes some way to resolving these issues. Each of these roles is described in general terms in the following sections, but students will have to use their institutions' regulations and procedures – in addition to discussion with supervisors – to establish who will do what in their examinations.

Examiners

Bearing in mind the fact that there may be as many variations in practice as there are institutions, it is likely that the audience at your oral examination will be a panel comprising internal and external examiners, your supervisor(s) (though not in all institutions) and/or a neutral chair (again, in some, not all, institutions). The one universal principle is that thesis and student are examined by someone who has not been involved in the project.

We can begin to define what each of these roles involves, but you should check exactly who will be there, what their titles are and what their roles are in your institution.

Once students become aware that their fate is in the hands of someone they are likely never to have met before, these are some of the questions that tend to flash through their minds:

- Who chooses the external examiner?
- How is this done?
- Can I have a say in who it will be?
- When is the best time to start thinking about this?
- How well should I know the examiner's work?
- What qualifications, experience or training should he or she have?
- Will my examiner be an expert in my area?
- How final should the examiner's copy of the thesis be?
- What are examiners looking for?
- Should I avoid arguing with them?

Should you know your examiner's work? It is not a bad idea to take a look at their publications – if you do not already know them – as this can give you insights on where they might be coming from in their questions. For example, if your examiner uses a completely different methodology from you, you might not have felt the need to include them in your literature review, but the examiner might want you to acknowledge the value of other methodologies, including the one(s) that he or she favours.

External examiners for the doctoral degree must have a doctorate themselves – usually, but there are exceptions. They will, in some sense, be experts. However, it is safe to assume that they will have had no training at all for this role. Although many who are new to the role report, informally, that they would appreciate guidance, if not training, traditionally, in the UK and elsewhere, external examiners have not been trained. There are, however, more recent moves by, for example, the Higher Education Funding Council for England, to change that. For the present, it is not a requirement: 'Examiners are not trained' (Wakeford 2002: 35); 'Training for examiners [is] to be available as part of the institution's staff development' (Metcalfe et al. 2002: 52). Even when training is provided – as the norm – it is doubtful that students will know in advance if their examiners have attended – and passed – such training.

The external examiner's main job is to write a report on the thesis before the oral examination takes place. They also, usually, complete an examiner's report during or after the oral examination. This report form requires the examiner to specify which criteria the student has, or has not, met during the oral examination and in the thesis. For example, there might be six or seven criteria, which might include 'The thesis is a record of original research' (at Strathclyde University). The examiner then has to tick each of the criteria that he or she judges that you have met during your examination. In addition, he or she will have to write down reasons for that judgement and for the outcome of your examination.

In some institutions students can have a say in the choice of external examiner. If this is the case in your institution, who should you choose? On the one hand, you want the best people in your field to be involved in your research. You may also want to involve the best people so that they get to know your work in detail; this could be useful later in your career. On the other hand, you might feel intimidated by the best people in your field, and they might actually have dominant personalities or behaviour styles. You may have heard from other students or colleagues that they tend to be intimidating as examiners. There may only be one expert in your field in any case, which makes the idea of 'choice' irrelevant. You should check how external examiners are chosen at your institution. This is best not left until the last minute, as the process of finding a date for the examination that suits everyone can take some time.

In some institutions, although the choice of external examiner is something that supervisors normally discuss with their students, it is not ultimately the candidate who makes the choice. In some places even the supervisor is excluded, the choice being made by a postgraduate director of the department. In practice, however, the supervisor often has a strong say in the choice, and he or she is often – not always – better placed to know who is likely to be sympathetic towards your approach or argument. It often happens that supervisors propose someone whom they know is a 'soft touch', someone who will not give you a hard time in your oral examination. This can, of course, misfire. Supervisors have – or have heard – tales of examiners who undergo personality change once they enter the doctoral examination.

Delamont et al. (1997) point out that selection of external examiners is not just about choosing the expert in your field. The choice is a balance of expertise in the area of research, qualifications and standing in the field, level of general knowledge of the field and, crucially, reputation as a fair examiner. They also add that the external examiner may be a useful ally or patron in a student's later career.

Many prefer experienced examiners, since they may have less to prove, and people from the higher education system, who understand the scale of the doctorate; they know what is involved and, some believe, are less likely to have unrealistic expectations. For those examiners who do not themselves have a doctorate, but have a wealth of relevant experience in another sector, for example, the supervisor may have to make a case to the institution for their appointment, specifying the proposed examiner's expertise. This might consist of a few lines detailing their relevant experience, i.e. relevant to examining a specific doctorate.

There are, therefore, informal procedures whereby potential examiners are 'researched', if they are not already known to supervisors or students – although they often are – and sounded out, in order to find out if they are willing and available to examine. There are also formal procedures, which differ from one institution to another, a general requirement being that the external is appointed by the university's senior academic decision-making committee, senate or board.

Examiners are not paid very much and often have informal reciprocal arrangements:

> For each PhD candidate two examiners are sought – one 'external', an established expert in the field, paid a paltry fee, and one 'internal', usually a member of the student's department who has played no significant part in the supervision. Potential externals are identified by the supervisor (sometimes in consultation with the student) and through a system of logrolling enticed to take on the duty – as a favour that it is anticipated will be returned.
>
> (Wakeford 2002: 35)

The key point here is that, in some institutions – not all – the student can discuss potential externals with the supervisor. They can suggest names. There may be instant agreement, or disagreement about who would make the best, easiest or fairest examiner, but there should be some discussion. This discussion should start well before the proposed date of the examination.

While the student is not always included in the selection of the external examiner, and many students are not even aware that they can have such involvement, there is a move to formalize the student's participation in selection: 'the student should . . . be able to comment on the choice of examiners' (Metcalfe et al. 2002: 52). In addition, Metcalfe et al. state that criteria for selection of both internal and external examiners should be 'transparent'.

The panel

This term is used to refer to the collective of the examiners (internal and external) and supervisor(s), but whether they will function *as a panel* is open to question. Will they, for example, make the pass/fail judgement as a panel, or does that decision rest with the external examiner at your institution?

While the use of the panel is standard practice in some institutions and cultures and a brand new concept in others, there has recently been a call for the panel to become standard practice: 'Final examination to be a viva with an independent panel of at least two examiners who are research active in relevant fields, at least one of whom is an external examiner' (Metcalfe et al. 2002: 52). Whether or not this becomes standard practice in the UK or elsewhere remains to be seen, but it is interesting to see the panel proposed so strongly. The strength of the panel model, particularly if it is managed by 'an independent chair', is that the examination would, in a sense, no longer be taking place 'behind closed doors'. In situations where participants fear the forces of nepotism and collusion, they might be reassured, although it is unlikely that their fear will be neutralized entirely. Nevertheless, since there are more people in the room, and since the external examiner does not chair the oral examination, there is a promise – though not a guarantee – of fairness. Presumably this is one of the purposes of this approach.

Roles

Students [spend] three years deferring to supervisors' judgements, striving to meet their expectations. So it came as a shock to discover that their supervisors were debarred from taking part in determining the outcome – which would be carried out by two people chosen for their unfamiliarity with the students' work . . . The position of the internal can . . . be delicate. Can they confidently contradict the view of their colleague's favoured and distinguished nominee in evaluating the work of that colleague's protégé?
(Wakeford 2002: 35)

In each institution there is the delicate question of who plays which role:

- Who is in charge?
- Who takes the lead?
- Who makes the final decision?
- Who has most power?
- Who will chair the viva?
- Will the supervisor ask questions or be silent?
- Who will keep a record of the discussion?

The last of these points is particularly important. On the day, you may want to check – either subtly or explicitly, by asking innocently – that the person allocated this role is, in fact, performing it.

The independent chair

In some universities a neutral person – i.e. neither supervisor nor examiner – chairs the oral examination. In some places this is standard practice, not only for the final examination, but also for regular doctoral review meetings. This role has been put in place to fulfil, potentially, several important functions. The independent chair has responsibility for ensuring the following:

- the assessment is rigorous, fair, reliable and consistent;
- the candidate has the opportunity to defend the thesis by ensuring that he or she has the opportunity to respond to all of the examiners' questions;
- the examiners' questioning is not aggressive, confrontational or inappropriate, by intervening, if required;
- examiners adhere to the institution's regulations and procedures, advising both examiners and candidate of regulations, as required;
- examiners' reports are completed prior to the examination.

This may or may not be the practice at your institution. Even if it is customary practice for doctoral progress reviews, you might want to check if the system will be continued at your oral examination. If there is no such system, the examination may be chaired by either the internal or external examiner. If the internal takes the role of chairing the examination, the external should lead with the questions.

While it might seem that adding another person to the examination increases pressure on students, in fact, candidates should be reassured that the independent chair's main role is to ensure that regulations and procedures are followed, and this can only be a good thing. Again, candidates will want to check how this role is described in their institutions.

Questions to ask at your institution

For some doctoral students, the definitions and guidance in this chapter will be self-evident; they will already have moved beyond the perspectives of thesis writer, researched the doctoral examination process in use at their institutions or happily be at institutions where doctoral examination practices are indeed 'transparent'. Even for these students, however, it might be as well to double check a few key points of information in advance.

Ask for information specific to the viva in your area/department. You presumably are not interested in hearing what people 'think about' the viva in general. You need information and, above all, current documentation from your institution and/or from your supervisor.

Questions to ask at your institution

- Where can I get a copy of the university's regulations, procedures and code of practice on the conduct of the doctoral examination?
- Who will my external examiner be? Has he or she been appointed by the university yet? If not, can I have a say in who should be asked?
- Who will attend my oral examination?
- What roles will each person play? What will each of them be looking for?
- How long is my oral examination likely to last?
- What will happen? Is there an agenda or protocol?
- Can I give a presentation?
- Can I have a copy of the examiner's report form to be used in my examination? Can I have a copy of the thesis report form that my examiner will use [if there is one]?
- Can I have a copy of the *Handbook for External Examiners* (UCoSDA)?
- When will I have a mock viva?

You should know whether or not your institution uses a two-stage doctoral examination process: in the first stage, the external examiner examines the thesis and writes a report on it; in the second stage, the external examiner writes a report, along with the internal examiner, at the end of the oral examination. You might want to ask what the regulations are about access to the examiner's report on the thesis:

> Very few institutions reported giving access to examiners' reports prior to the viva. Yet it is arguable that there is some merit in, at the very least, giving students an insight into the kinds of issues that are likely to arise at the viva and conversely, perhaps, little merit in keeping those issues secret until the viva itself. The question of what information should be passed to students prior to their oral examination must be answered in the context of the institutional view of the purposes of the viva as part of the entire examination process and particularly the way in which it acts as an opportunity to defend an intellectual position (a thesis) ... In short, institutions might wish to discuss if their primary aim in setting the style of the viva is to test candidates' abilities to defend their work in an immediate and to some degree spontaneous way – in short by being put on the spot? If the answer is yes then clearly a system that gives no prior information regarding issues to be discussed is appropriate; however, if this answer is no (or is less equivocal) then a rethinking or what is to be made available prior to the viva may be appropriate.
>
> (Powell and Brown 2007: 17)

Clearly, this will be a contested area, but doctoral students can ask what the practice is at their institutions and might benefit from reading the full report from which the above quotation is extracted. Even if they do not have access to the examiner's report on their own theses, this report might shed some light on the potential content of such reports.

Questions to ask your supervisor

- Does the department have procedures for the doctoral examination? If so, can I have a copy?
- How long will my oral examination last?
- Who will be there?
- What types of question can I expect?
- How do I assess whether or not my answer is correct?
- What if I cannot answer the examiner's question?
- Do I have to say how my thesis fits into the broader picture?
- Can I assume by this stage that I have passed?
- How much background knowledge do I need?
- Where should I set the limits?
- Where can I go just before the examination starts?
- Who is on my side?
- Will you be there?
- Will anyone help me if I get into problems?
- What should I wear?
- If I do badly in the oral examination, but my thesis is good, will I pass?
- What is the standard I have to achieve?
- Should I admit the weaknesses of the study?

Be prepared to repeat your questions, to ask follow-up questions or to ask your questions in different ways. Do not be content with the answer 'it depends'.

Audit your existing skills

Lest we forget, students have an active role at this stage too: to prepare themselves to perform well on the day. While Chapter 8 provides a framework for practice, this is a good point to consider the implications of what has been covered in this chapter for your conduct during your oral examination. This is a time to take stock of your strengths and weaknesses in oral discussions:

- Are you good at giving oral presentations?
- What are your strengths?
- Do you have any weaknesses?
- Have you found it easy/difficult to understand questions about your work in that context?
- Do you think you have answered them well in the past?
- Have you had any feedback on your performances?
- Have you performed well under pressure?
- Have you performed well in the face of negative or aggressive questioning?

This is not a time to revert to the 'ostrich' position described at the start of this chapter; instead, it is time to face up to areas where you have to work out how best to engage with the participants – and their different roles – in your oral examination.

Checklist

- Roles and responsibilities at your oral examination: who will be there, and what will they do?
- Regulations and procedures: get the latest versions. Check your department too.
- Which oral skills do you already have? What skills will you need to improve?

4

Countdown to your examination

Expectations • At the start of the doctorate • Three months before your examination • One month to go • One week to go • The day before • On the day • Thirty minutes before your examination • During • After • Preparation schedule • Checklist

The previous chapters aimed to provide insights into what to expect in an oral examination. In this chapter, we jump to the stages when the examination is becoming imminent. It now has a fixed date, and your time for preparation is limited. At this time most students have other responsibilities and duties, and many will be working during this period. In these circumstances it is easy to lose track of time. All the more reason to place the preparation process in real time and to set interim deadlines for the different types of preparation that are required. If you are going to need other people to help you prepare, you must get their time committed well in advance. If you are to perform at your best on the day of the examination, nothing should be left to the last minute or even, it could be argued, to the last month.

This chapter offers guidance in planning the preparation, prompting students – and supervisors – to structure their preparation as a process of learning, revising and, for some, honing skills. This time management approach is also a strategy for managing rising stress levels at this stage (Droogleever Fortuyn et al. 2004).

The word 'countdown', in the simple sense counting backwards from a fixed point in time, as in '10 . . . 9 . . . 8 . . .', is used here to emphasize that all the very different aspects of preparation must be planned in real time. If you have a countdown towards your examination, you can be clear about where you are in relation to the event. You can then plan the different types of checks and preparation that you need to do at each stage. To assist this planning process, a preparation schedule is provided at the end of this chapter.

Good supervisors will help their students to plan their preparation carefully, but students can be active, rather than passive, in the countdown. Instead of watching the months and weeks slide by, students should structure their preparations so that they feel more ready and more competent as the day of the examination approaches.

Expectations

Students should start by reviewing their expectations:

- Based on all the information you have collected so far (see previous chapter), and based on all the discussions you have had with your supervisor(s) and others, what do you think is likely to happen in your examination?
- What do you know for a fact will happen?
- What are you still unsure about?

Some students find it helpful to write down any remaining issues or questions, thereby possibly beginning to confront them, giving them more definition but certainly giving you a chance to face up to them. If, on the other hand, you choose not to write them down, the risk is that questions continue to swim around in your head and may remain insufficiently defined for you to deal with them.

This is, of course, arguable – everyone is different – but the tactic of putting your expectations down on paper is worth trying. At the very least, it helps you prepare for discussions with your supervisor. In addition to checking aspects you are unsure about, it might be worth checking on aspects of your viva that you think you can be quite sure about.

The next step is to discuss emerging issues with your supervisor: does he or she agree with your view? Discussing your and their expectations can have a crucial corrective function: if you have any faulty expectations, your supervisor can tell you right away. If you do not have this discussion, how will you know? You will also, potentially, have extra 'uncertainty baggage'; for any issues that you have not checked you will have several more uncertainties to take with you into the examination. Some students report that they are simply too afraid to ask about certain aspects of their examination. They would rather not think about it.

On the other hand, there are students who are much more secure about what is expected of them and their ability to provide it on the day, but even they will surely see the sense of *checking* their 'certainties'. It is possible for even the brightest people to have a false sense of security.

These steps allow you to externalize your expectations, to examine them in the company of someone who knows more about doctoral examinations – we hope – than you do. This is your opportunity to review your understanding of what will and will not happen and, if need be, to reshape your expectations. Expectations, whatever their origins – and that in itself would be an interesting piece of research – are not constant.

The emotional dimension of preparing for the oral examination may come in here too. As the word 'countdown' suggests, some – perhaps most – students find that their anxiety levels increase as the day of their examination draws closer. This is perfectly understandable, but the point is that each student has to find some way of coping with that tension. On the other hand, if you cannot see what all the talk of mounting tension is about, perhaps it will be, for you, more a matter of motivating yourself for your examination. You still have work to do, after all, to persuade your examiner that your work meets the required standards.

If you are in the unfortunate position – for many possible, understandable and unavoidable reasons – of having little or no time to prepare, scan the earlier sections of this chapter and concentrate on the later stages of the countdown.

If you feel that you do not have enough time, *do not panic*. Do not get angry with your supervisor for not forcing you to spend more time preparing. Do not waste energy on 'what you might/should have done'. Focus on the time that you have. Prioritize. Check that the wheels of the system are turning. Spend as much time as you can practising.

If you are reading this the night before your viva, it might be a better idea to skip this chapter and go to the chapters on questions (5) and answers (6) and to use these selectively to practise now.

At the start of the doctorate

It could be argued that it is never too early to start thinking about your examination (Trafford and Leshem 2008). While each doctorate is different, there is only one set of procedures used in each examination in each institution. These procedures include the criteria that will be used in the examination. It is possible, therefore, to find out which criteria will be used to evaluate your work. (See Chapters 2 and 3 for directions on this point.)

Find the examiner's report form currently used at your university. Check that this is the form to be used in your oral examination. The form will make explicit the criteria your examiners will use during your examination. This may, in turn, influence aspects of your research and writing. The criteria – along with the university's higher degree regulations (or whatever they are called at your institution) – give an idea of what is expected in the thesis you are about to write.

Three months before your examination

This is the point in time before the examination when students submit their theses. You will already have given your supervisors the full and final draft of all your chapters, but make sure you give them the most recent copy, identical to the version that will be, or has been, sent to the external examiner.

Plan your oral examination practice sessions. Set a date, time and place. Who will take part? Who will play the role of external examiner? Find out about your external examiner. What has he or she written lately? How does his or her perspective relate to yours? What types of question is your examiner likely to ask? What can you say about this examiner's work or approach?

Read your institution's doctoral examination procedures and criteria. It is time to relate these criteria to the work of your doctorate and to your thesis. You can do this in discussion with your supervisor:

- To what extent does your thesis meet some/all of the criteria?
- How will you meet the criteria in your performance during your oral examination?
- To what extent, if at all, will these criteria be used to evaluate the work you did throughout the doctorate?

There may be other aspects of the examiner's form that you want to discuss:

- When will it be filled in?
- Will you see it or be given a copy?
- Where does it go once it has been filled in?

If you know exactly how the paperwork is meant to work, you will be able to check on its progress through the system. This is particularly important for those students who have to graduate by a certain date. If you have a specific graduation date in mind, make sure everyone involved knows that. At an appropriate moment, during the final examination discussions, for example, you can ask if it is feasible for you – and the paperwork – to make that date.

It is up to you to check that the wheels of the system are turning:

- Have your internal and external examiners been approved by the faculty board, or whatever group has to initially approve them? If not, remember that this could delay the whole process.

- Have the examiners been approved by the university senate, or whatever body approves them in your institution? There can be no examination until the external examiner has been formally approved by the university.
- Has your thesis been sent to the external examiner? Any delay here will delay your examination. The external examiner needs a certain amount of time, specified in your university's procedures/regulations, to read a thesis.
- Has the date for your oral examination been formally approved?
- Has the external examiner agreed to that date? In writing?
- Has the internal examiner likewise agreed?
- Does your supervisor have it in his or her diary?

One month to go

Re-read

As you re-read your thesis, do not just read it from start to finish as if it were a book. Instead, write a one-sentence summary of each chapter. These sentences will act as prompts for later recall and discussion.

Revise

Who are the four or five key people in your field? Revise their names and details of their work:

- What were their key papers/books?
- Which publications had most influence on your work?
- When were they published? Dates? Published in which journals or by which publishers?

All of this, and more, will be in your thesis. The point is not that you should be doing new reading – although you probably will and can mention that at the examination – but that you should revise the reading you have done to the extent that you are able to talk about selected publications in detail.

Link

Can you make direct connections with topics you are likely to talk about or that you will introduce into the discussion, i.e. prepare to introduce topics that you want to discuss?

Highlight

What are the highlights of your thesis? Where exactly are they? In which chapters? You can mark these in some way, e.g. with yellow 'stickies'. You can, of course, make sure the markers are facing you, on the day of the examination, and are only visible to you. Even better, memorize where they are, i.e. which pages they are on. The best strategy is to practise talking about these highlights so often that you know exactly what and where they are. You will then have no need to mark them. More importantly, you will be 'fluent' in talking about them.

To some students this seems like a huge burden, but once you have identified six or seven key pages, and once you have practised referring to them in discussions and mock vivas, you will find that you can easily and fluently refer to them. Some students feel that they should not mark areas of the text, that this seems like, and will be seen as, cheating. Perhaps this is just another symptom of the general sense of disempowerment that the doctoral examination creates for some students. Perhaps it is an indicator of how passively many doctoral students approach their own examinations, judging their best course of action to be to follow the examiner's lead in all things (even when they are not sure where the examiner is likely to lead them). Some students are not even aware that they can take their thesis in with them to their examinations and refer to it while giving their answers. Some feel that they are not at liberty to open it until the examiner says they can. Perhaps this type of expectation shows students' fear of taking responsibility for lines of discussion; although students know that they are responsible for their answers, they still feel constrained in terms of what is the 'right way to behave' and what is the 'right answer'. Sadly, there may be no clear indicators of 'right answers' on the day.

Students can practise taking the initiative in discussion of their work. Surely, you must find a way to discuss the highlights of your work. If so, then you should practise discussing these highlights and making a convincing case for them *as highlights*. You must practise finding connections between these highlights and any type of question that the examiners ask. Making such connections may take practice. This need not take up a lot of your time, but it should involve several iterations, as you practise with different forms of question.

Above all, remember to answer the question, since examiners want you to answer their questions, not to go off on some 'riff' in which you sing your own praises.

Check

You will have checked the text of your thesis many times. Now is the time to check it even more carefully. If you know someone who is good at proofreading now is the time to ask them for a big favour.

1 Correct typographical and other errors.
2 Check cross-referencing from one chapter to another.
3 Check tables, graphs, etc. Are they all numbered correctly?

Type out a list of corrections. It is not universal practice to give such a list to the examiner, but it could be considered good practice for the student, since it indicates in black and white how thorough you have been in your checking. This may defuse any frustration or impatience that your examiner might feel at any errors that you let slip into the draft that they have been reading.

Describe

Can you describe your doctoral experience in a coherent way? You could represent it as narrative, a learning process, a series of decisions made along the way, a sequence of milestones in your research, a series of problems solved or a natural progression from your undergraduate degree.

Update

Read recent literature in your specific area. Update your knowledge. Have any of the key figures in your field, referred to in your thesis, published any books or papers since you completed your thesis?

Write

Write sample questions. Rehearse answers. Rehearse many times, even with different people.

Practise

Have a mock viva. Practise what you – and your supervisor – expect to happen in your examination.

Put together a 'viva kit'

What will you take with you into your examination?

- Your thesis.
- Blank paper.
- Several pens or pencils.
- Laptop?
- Printouts?
- Water?

Stress

You already have stress management skills, such as setting realistic goals, working with support and allies, understanding what is required of you and how you can achieve it and ways of dealing with pressure. If you have not had time to work on each of these in relation to your oral examination, be sure to work quickly on them with someone you trust, someone who knows about doctoral examinations. Use all of your usual self-esteem building tricks. Call on all your positive, supportive friends and colleagues.

What about managing your stress on the day? Practise breathing between sentences and within sentences, as you speak. Decide on a relaxed posture to adopt – one that you are comfortable with. Practise taking your time to construct detailed answers. Practise not looking for positive feedback to your answers. Remind yourself that you are being examined on your thesis; the answers to almost all the questions are there – and in your memory – already.

One week to go

Practise using the oral examination strategies outlined in Chapters 5 and 6. The two key strategies for answers are 'start with the thesis' and 'define-defend'. The first will help you to focus on specifics and the second will stop you becoming defensive.

- Practise oral summaries: long and short.
- Practise oral debate.
- Visit the room where your examination will be held. Check the layout. Think about/find out how it will be set out for your examination. Practise in that room, if you can. Check where everyone is likely to sit, if you can. If not, practise in a similar room, with your 'mock examiners' sitting in different seats. Practise being asked to wait outside the room and then brought in by one of your 'mock examiners'.
- Decide where you will wait just before the examination.
- Get a viva kit: thesis, paper, pens, water, etc.
- What will you wear? Is it clean? Does it still fit? Does it all match? Are you comfortable wearing it?
- Relax, exercise, eat and sleep well.
- Negotiate temporary, one-week unconditional support from friends, peers, family and partner.
- Can you cancel or postpone any duties and commitments in the week leading up to your examination, particularly on the day before your examination?

• Plan back up transport, childcare, clothing, support, cash, etc. in case something goes wrong on the day.

The day before

Eat and sleep well. Take best care of yourself. Have as many treats as you like. Visualize yourself doing well in your viva. Take time off. If you are worried about not sleeping well, have a nap during the day.

L'enfer, c'est les autres.

(Sartre 1945)

Sartre's play tells us that 'hell is other people'. For this particular day, there might be more truth in this than many would otherwise, on other days, admit. Today is the day to let no one make any demands on you, unless, of course, you like the idea of being distracted by other people, so that you do not obsess about your examination.

• Avoid people in whose company you feel anxious or irritated.
• Stay out of the way of people with whom you feel intimidated or undermined.
• Spend time with positive, supportive people.
• Focus on the strengths of your work and writing.
• Spend your last 24 pre-examination hours with people who help you do that.

At this time, the company of someone who can make you laugh would be no bad thing. This might release some of your tension. There is such a thing as being too uptight about the examination.

On the day

Use your best routine:

• Your best wake-up routine is . . .
• Company and conversation? Or not?
• Perhaps best not to read a new journal article or book chapter.
• Transport? Worth booking a taxi? Organizing a lift/ride?
• Eat a real breakfast, and/or take food with you.

- Leave plenty of time for everything.
- Check you have everything you need for your examination.
- Get there early . . . how early?

Thirty minutes before your examination

- Relax. Breathe. Drink water. Think positively. Breathe again.
- Focus on the task ahead. Write notes on your strengths.
- Do not wander off. Wait until they come and get you.
- Only engage in spontaneous conversation if that suits you.
- Likewise phone calls and e-mails: are they a useful or unsettling distraction?

During

- Keep breathing. Slow down your speech. Speak carefully.
- Look at the examiners as you answer their questions.
- Write down their questions. Write notes for your answers.
- Talk about your thesis. Refer to the work you did.
- Nod. Smile. Look at your notes. Breathe.

After

Make sure you leave the room knowing exactly what corrections you need to make to your thesis (if any). These may be provided in a promised report from the examiner. Ask your examiner to specify the scale and scope of revisions, if you can. For example, if you are asked to add something, what does that mean? Add a sentence? A paragraph? A page? Or more? If need be, rephrase your questions and ask follow-up questions till you get specific answers. The more you define the writing tasks before the end of your examination, the less you will have to think about them, and the easier it will be to get them done.

If you have only minor corrections/revisions to do, do them as soon as possible. It will be easier to do them while they are still fresh in your mind. If you leave them even a couple of weeks, then you will have to review what you were asked to do.

Do not forget the final rituals. Although you may not call yourself 'Doctor' until you have graduated, you have, to all intents and purposes, 'passed'.

If, on the other hand, you have not had a good outcome, why not go ahead with the proposed celebrations anyway? These will, in any case, be difficult to cancel, and it will do you good to hear people's positive views of you and, possibly, negative views of examiners.

Remember that with the examination over, you are losing a large part of your life. Paradoxically, this can be a loss and/or grieving process. All the more reason to have some form of celebration, or several. If you are very lucky, you will have a good friend or partner to organize such an event for you.

- Relax, rest, play and celebrate – you've earned it.
- Thank your supporters and allies – they have too.

Preparation schedule

Draw up a preparation schedule as follows.

Preparation schedule		
	Task	Time
At the start of the doctorate	....	....
Three months pre-examination	....	....
One month pre-examination	....	....
One week to go	....	....
The day before	....	....
On the day	....	....
Thirty minutes before the examination starts	....	....
During the examination	....	....
After the examination	....	....

Checklist

- Plan your preparations in real time. Write real dates in the above schedule.
- Get help and support – who will give you general support, who will help you practise? You will need to put them in this schedule too.
- Do practice sessions at every stage in the countdown.

5

Questions

> Whether the setting be home, place of work, or classroom, questions initiate learning. They can excite, disturb, discipline, or comfort, but always stimulate inquiry.
>
> (Christensen et al. 1991: 156)

The prospect of the questions that will be asked in the oral examination fills many students with curiosity and some doctoral students with fear. For those who know their subject well, the questions can indeed 'excite', just as any other deep conversation with experts in the field can. What might 'disturb' is the taking apart of a thesis that the candidate has so carefully put together into an integrated whole. Yet there is satisfaction to be found in the discipline of subjecting a piece of work to close scrutiny. It is also possible, if the questions are predicted and answers are practised, to find some 'comfort' in the questions. In the context of the oral examination, questioning can stimulate inquiry, but the emphasis should, at least initially, be on examination of the work done.

This chapter provides an analysis of the types of questions that come up in doctoral examinations. This is not to say that the examination consists of a series of simple question-and-answer exchanges. More complex interactions also occur. These questions are drawn from many years of discussions with supervisors, examiners and students, and therefore represent more types of question than are likely to come up in any one examination. How predictable are doctoral examination questions? Some argue, based on anecdote and experience, that the questions asked will be different in each discipline. However, there is evidence of 'clusters' of questions that can be predicted (Trafford and Leshem 2002b) and should be used to prepare.

For the individual student preparing for his or her examination, the aim of this chapter is to help you to work out how you are going to approach the task of answering questions, in general, and how you are going to answer the types of questions that come up specifically. For example, what approach do you see yourself taking in your answers? What tone do you want to strike: reflective, confrontational or educational? If you are challenged, how will you respond? Will you maintain the tone of dialogue or debate? Strategies for answering doctoral examination questions will be provided in the next chapter.

While many of the questions covered in this chapter are, quite deliberately, written in general terms, it is the student's responsibility to write forms of these questions that are much more specific to his or her thesis and research, as appropriate.

For more developed questions, i.e. some that are longer and more detailed, see Trafford and Leshem (2008).

Naturally, you should talk with your supervisor(s) about both the general and specific forms of likely examination questions.

Since it is unlikely that *all* of these questions will come up in your examination, you will need to compile your 'set' of questions and plan your practice sessions around them.

The most important purpose of questions – both in theory, in this chapter, and in your examination – is to stimulate your learning. Learning what? – learning how much you have learned since you started your doctorate. The questions asked in your examination will help you to appreciate this quite acutely, but it might be as well to start that learning before you enter your examination. In other words, the thinking and practising that will be prompted by the questions covered in this chapter are intended to help you to get some of that learning done before you enter your examination.

Review your doctoral 'history'

A good way to begin your examination preparation is to think back over the course of your doctoral studies. Recall the topics you discussed with your supervisor, particularly those that he or she seemed to want to discuss regularly, or repeatedly. Remember the feedback you received at earlier stages in your work:

Review feedback

- Were there any signals about elements of your work that were or are stronger or weaker than others?
- Did feedback on a particular chapter, paper or report you wrote seem especially positive?
- Did anything you did, said or wrote create a strong negative or sceptical response?
- Were you ever surprised by the amount of time your supervisor seemed to want to spend discussing some aspect of your work?
- Which questions were you asked at the proposal stage and during the research design, data gathering and analysis stages? Were there any recurring questions that never seemed to go away?
- Which questions were you asked at conferences and seminars? Which areas of your work or your writing strike audiences or readers as most contentious, interesting and/or valuable?
- What questions did your supervisor ask you in the last few months of your doctoral work? What comments did they make on later versions and final drafts of your chapters?

The aim of these questions is to jog your memory: there may be potential examination questions in your doctoral history. Alternatively, there may be signals in these earlier discussions about what is likely to come up in your examination discussions. There may even be patterns, recurring questions over recent months, that you can see once you analyse these discussions. These patterns might have seemed to you, at the time, as no more than your supervisor's personal fixations, but they may now indicate where debate is likely to occur. In addition, questions you have already been asked may indicate the reactions examiners are likely have to your work and the types of questions they will ask.

If you have trouble remembering that far back, you could try using my 'emerging topology of supervisors' comments' in *How to Write a Thesis* (Murray 2006) to jog your memory. If, however, you cannot remember any questions, or if you have not presented your work often, or have not discussed it with your supervisor often enough, or recently enough, to know what they think about your work now, then you can try asking your supervisor to cast his or her mind back in order to recover a few questions.

Alternatively, it may be that questions that have recurred throughout your doctoral history can be considered to have been thoroughly answered; perhaps you should concentrate on new questions. Remember, however, that the examiners will not be aware of all the subjects and questions you have discussed with your supervisor. You may have to answer those very familiar questions all over again. Try to recall your best answers, reflect on whether or not there has been any progression in your answers: for example, have they become stronger over time? Have they changed subtly or radically over time? Showing your awareness of the inadequacy of your earlier answers – and the strength of your 'newer' answers – is one way of demonstrating both your knowledge and your learning. You can explicitly compare earlier and later answers to make this very clear.

> At the end of the day, you will have to decide for yourself how to generate questions and which ones, generated by others, including this book, are relevant to your examination and useful for your practice sessions.

Another purpose of preparing an overview of your doctoral experience is to prepare you for what is frequently the first question:

- Why did you choose this topic for doctoral study (Trafford and Leshem 2002b: 41)?
- How did you develop an interest in this subject?
- Could you tell us a bit about how you came to do this research?
- What made you want to do research on this?
- I'd like to know what the origins of this thesis were for you.

Your answer could take many forms:

- Theoretical, based on your previous studies or research.
- Personal, drawing on your long-standing commitment to the subject.
- Professional, growing out of your experience and networks.
- Conceptual, based on where your work is currently located in the discipline.

Do not worry if, during your answer, one of the examiners stares at the floor; he or she may simply be thinking about the first 'serious' question they are going to ask next or about how to link it to what you are saying; or even about what he or she is going to have for dinner. There is no way you can work out what they are thinking as you are answering. So there is all the more reason to prepare answers with which you are satisfied, so as not to be thrown by the apparent responses – or lack of responses – of examiners.

The predictable and the unpredictable

While this chapter will help you to anticipate the types of questions that could be asked in your examination, it should be pointed out, at the outset, that it is not possible for you – or anyone else – to anticipate all the questions, or, equally importantly, the forms that those questions will take on the day. While certain elements are predictable, there will still be an element of unpredictability. Having said that, if there are, as Trafford and Leshem (2002b) have found, recurring questions, then perhaps it is much less predictable than we are led to believe. In fact, they argue that clusters of recurring questions – across a range of doctoral examinations that they attended as part of their study – can be taken to represent a 'template' not only for preparing for the examination, but also for writing the thesis. In other words, recurring questions indicate what could be seen as core criteria for the doctorate: 'Although the questions did not always use similar words, nonetheless they sought explanations from candidates on similar aspects of their doctoral thesis' (Trafford and Leshem 2002b: 36). Based on a knowledge of these – or other – recurring questions, students could draw up their own template for their examinations. Such a template could – and arguably should – be based on the criteria for the examination, such as were defined in Chapter 2. As Trafford and Leshem (2002b) argue, examiners will expect to work through the criteria in some fashion and will expect students to demonstrate, in their responses, that they meet their university's criteria. 'Criteria' will therefore almost definitely mean local criteria; since examiners have to fill in your university's form and follow your university's procedures, they have to use your university's criteria in judging your work and performance.

However, even if you do anticipate thoroughly everything that is likely to be asked, it is equally likely that the behaviour of the examiners will affect you right from the start:

> A generally abrupt demeanour adopted by the interviewer would produce greater psychological distance . . . Participants tested in the 'abrupt' condition gained higher scores for Shift and Total Suggestibility than those in the 'friendly' condition . . . Whilst initial responses to leading questions are mediated by more stable cognitive factors that are relatively unaffected by interviewer demeanour, post-feedback scores may be more sensitive to the social aspects of suggestibility.
>
> (Bain and Baxter 2000: 123)

What this means is that the *style* of the questions could influence your answers. Some would argue that what Bain and Baxter (2000) refer to as 'psychological distance' is appropriate for the doctoral examination; others would say that style is very much up to the examiner, meaning that the candidate is unlikely to know what exactly to expect until the examination starts.

Do we really have enough knowledge of these processes? It has to be noted, for example, that while psychological distance might be deemed appropriate, it can have the effect of increasing pressure on the interviewee. Do examiners consider the pros and cons of the style they adopt? For example, are they fully aware of the potential impact of adopting a 'friendly' style by, for example, smiling at the candidate when he or she enters the room at the start of the examination? Perhaps they do know this and use such tactics to gain an advantage, to manipulate the student's level of anxiety. Such aspects of non-verbal communication will be considered trivial by some supervisors, students and examiners; however, as long as they do not undermine the student's performance, and as long as the student is able to be sufficiently attuned to non-verbal cues and sufficiently strong to hold their own in an argument, even the most 'abrupt' style will not throw them.

While Bain and Baxter's (2000) research is not based on the doctoral examination context, we can learn lessons from it that are relevant to the doctoral examination: the behaviour of examiners can influence your answers to their questions. Their actions, tone and non-verbal communication can, it seems certain, have an impact on your coping strategies, particularly if you are feeling under immense pressure and even vulnerable in your oral examination, as many do:

> All witnesses, victims and suspects enter an interrogation with a general cognitive set regarding the situation. This cognitive set is influenced by uncertainty about the subject-matter of the interrogation . . . This general cognitive set can facilitate either a resistant or suggestible behavioural response to the interrogation.
>
> (Bain and Baxter 2000: 124)

This raises the question of what constitutes a – or your – 'cognitive set'. Even if you feel that you have no such thing, there is bound to be a set of beliefs about the examination and the examiner that will influence your behaviour. If your set of beliefs is confirmed or confounded in the opening minutes of your examination, or at some later stage, how will you react? Can you practise that? How vulnerable are you to interpersonal pressure – not just to cognitive or theoretical pressure? Can you practise this kind of interpersonal pressure?

What are the implications for the student in an oral examination? While the research quoted here focuses on eyewitness reliability in the context of a criminal investigation, there may be aspects of such studies that can teach us something about how we behave as interviewees, when subjected to similar pressures. For example, the study found that negative feedback can have two effects: it can make subjects change their previous responses or it can increase their suggestibility to subsequent leading questions. From this we can infer that if you accept negative feedback, you may find that this leads to knock-on cognitive and/or affective effects, such as decreased self-esteem, increased anxiety and – even more complicated – increased susceptibility to perceiving weaknesses in your work. As this reaction sets in, it brings with it a further shift in perception: 'making [you] more likely to attend to external cues rather than relying on [your] own internal frame of reference' (Bain and Baxter 2000: 124). This provides one explanation of how it is that we can be moved – or let ourselves be moved – from our own internal frame of reference.

This is an interesting psychological process that has not been fully researched in the context of the doctoral examination, but it seems sensible to consider research in this area, since it offers potential insights into the thought processes of interviewees. In discussions with examiners, supervisors and students some say that this type of material is irrelevant; others see it as directly, unexpectedly, parallel to their experiences of doctoral examinations. While the question of relevance should continue to be a matter of debate, there are, for some, striking echoes of examination experiences:

> Compliance occurs . . . when interviewees give in to what they perceive is required of them in an attempt to appease interviewers and avoid confrontation, so that they yield to suggestions and change their responses during the procedure, even if they know privately that their answer is wrong. A tendency to compliance may also forestall memory search and retrieval processes.
>
> (Bain and Baxter 2000: 124)

This quotation begins to make sense of narratives about oral examinations in which 'it all goes horribly wrong'. Rather than generally attributing a student's inarticulateness to the tension of the examination, or bullying by the examiner, we must look more closely at the relationship between students' desire to avoid confrontation with a leading scholar and their ensuing demonstration of diminished ability to access their memories. Again, in the context of the doctoral examination, it has to be said that there is plenty of research to be done here. It would be interesting, for example, to study the actual interventions in oral examinations, to assess whether or not this pattern occurs there. There are also implications here for the training of examiners. However, for students preparing for their examinations, there is plenty of preparation that can continue on the basis of the current level of knowledge: identifying the potential side-effects of negative criticism and developing strong answers remain priorities.

In the context of an oral examination, negative feedback will, at least, give the student food for thought. Negative feedback will raise questions – perhaps expected, perhaps unexpected – about the work or the thesis. This is not to say that all students will, or should, cave in under negative feedback; on the contrary, they clearly have to defend their work, as far as it can be defended. In fact, one effect of negative feedback can be to stimulate students to be more critical, to make them rise to the challenge of defending their work. Moreover, if the negative feedback is unexpected, or if the style in which it is given is unexpected, then students will have to be careful to avoid the outcomes documented in Bain and Baxter's (2000) study.

Finally, the study concludes with a consideration of the possibility of 'standard technique' (Bain and Baxter 2000: 132). As Bain and Baxter point out, before we can have such, we would have to analyse existing practices in ways that have not, as yet, been possible. In the context of the doctoral examination, of course, there is no such thing as 'standard technique', nor would there be general agreement that there should be, for reasons rehearsed elsewhere in this book. In fact, there is a great deal of investigation to be done before anything approaching that could be generated. In the meantime, many students are left facing a high degree of unpredictability.

Of all the expected and unexpected elements of the oral examination, it would seem logical and reasonable to assume that we know ourselves well. However, under pressure, particularly interpersonal pressure, we may behave in unpredictable ways. Psychologists may find this section all too familiar, but the rest of us may be learning about these aspects of our personality for the first time. The doctoral examination is a new kind of interaction with authority, and it should be assumed that it can bring out the unexpected in us. However, the study summarized in this section offers a framework for understanding our behaviours, for avoiding acting out our vulnerability and for maintaining our 'cognitive set'.

Having identified the competing aspects of predictability and unpredictability in this section, we can consider the nature of the doctoral 'interrogation' more specifically. The following sections identify recurring types of questions, while strategies for developing effective answers are dealt with in the next chapter.

Putting the student at ease

I had expected more of a preamble, and I was starting cold. I hadn't got the feel of them at all. I glanced at Brown. He gave me a smile of recognition, but his eyes were wary and piercing behind his spectacles. There was no give there. He was sitting back, his jowls swelling over his collar, as in a portrait of an eighteenth-century bishop.

(Snow 1960: 204)

Some examiners like their first words to strike a note of humour or reassurance. They may say something completely irrelevant – to the examination – or inconsequential, as they introduce themselves. The purpose of this may be to make them seem more human and less intimidating to the candidate, whom they assume to be nervous. Another tack is to reassure the candidate that standards of fairness will be observed during the examination. There may be some discussion about how the examination will be conducted. The examiner may introduce everyone, even though most already know each other.

However, we know that there are examiners who feel that candidates are sufficiently mature – or should be – to manage their own anxiety levels. These examiners may feel that a certain amount of tension is appropriate, or unavoidable. There are some who will not take time to put you at your ease. There may even be one or two who will want to see how you cope with the situation. Many will consider such approaches unfair, but it does happen. On the other hand, it might not be intended to put you under pressure: the examiner may simply feel under pressure of time, whether this is because he or she has to make a flight back or has to meet some other deadline.

Whether or not examiners *consciously* adopt one of these modes is, as with so much of the doctoral examination, open to question. For the student, therefore, it is as well to be ready for both types of examiner: the one who puts you at your ease and the one who gets straight down to the business of examination. Whatever the examiner does and says, it is up to you to manage your thoughts and feelings at this stage. You are unlikely, in any case, to feel truly 'at ease', but you can develop ways to stop your anxiety getting the better of you. You can, of course, practise responding to the various opening remarks, asking your 'mock examiners' to use a range of different forms in your practice sessions.

Small talk

There may be some initial banter, initiated by the examiner, the supervisor or the internal, about the venue, the journey, the weather, the coffee or any aspect of the meeting, other than its real subject. The aim of this may be to let you start talking in a 'low stakes' kind of way. Some students find this annoying, as they feel time is wasted that could be spent discussing the thesis. Others are more philosophical, or opportunistic, depending on your point of view, and are quite happy to see examination time taken up with such easy subjects. These discussions may take the form of questions, so it might be as well to have some sociable, enthusiastic or neutral answers ready.

If something to eat is provided, such as scones, only eat if you know that you do not have to speak for a minute or so, although in one doctoral examination the – substantial – scones were themselves an initial talking point. In the USA, we would have to call them biscuits; in the UK, of course, that means something else, and this too may be a topic of opening chat.

How you follow, and whether you initiate, such small talk is, of course, a matter of personality and, perhaps, reading the situation. Do they appear to expect you to add anything to the conversation or not? The safe advice would be to follow their lead, and to keep what you say pretty light, neutral and brief. Small talk, in this context, does not mean gossip, not for you anyway: stay away from such topics as colleagues or peers – either in your institution or elsewhere – even if the examiner starts talking about them. Unless the discussion is purely academic – i.e. about others' research – this might be risky.

Establishing rapport

Establishing rapport is usually the purpose of such opening remarks, questions and conversational asides. Does it matter? Surely, what matters is the quality of your work, rather than your and the examiners' social skills? Surely, what matters is the examiners' expertise in your area, not their ability to generate appropriate small talk and establish rapport with you? Some would question whether or not rapport is truly achievable in this context. It could also be argued – and it might be felt by some examiners – that it is inappropriate to establish rapport in a doctoral examination, as it might undermine the examiner's neutrality. The examiner might be conscious of the need to leave you free to give answers that you choose, without being influenced – consciously or unconsciously – by his or her reactions.

The quality of rapport between examiner and candidate might not matter much to you, but it is important to follow the cues. You do not necessarily have to go into detail, but it is appropriate to give brief, positive responses when prompted. There is no point in responding to rapport-building prompts or questions with impatience or surprise. It serves no purpose to reveal your reluctance to answer any question put to you in your examination, even this type. In any case, harder questions will surely follow soon enough.

Another approach is to consider what you can learn about the examiner from how he or she behaves, puts you at your ease and makes the transition to more focused discussion. Experienced examiners are often quite skilled in these processes. While they may not go as far as demonstrating empathy for your position or admiration of your work, they may have quite subtle strategies like talking directly to you, rather than just to the internal and your supervisor, pausing to give you time to reply, so that you can see if your voice is still working, or stating their shared interest in your subject. However obvious, this has the potential to establish some kind of affinity, rather than adversity, between candidate and examiner. This can sometimes set the tone – possibly for all participants – for the rest of your examination.

Questions about you

Examiners may move from this superficial chat to questions that seem more personal. They may ask you about your experience, your education, your interests and your networks. The purpose of these questions may still be to ease you into a more probing discussion, but they may also mark a transition into talking about your research.

Examiners may also ask you about your research training, any experience you have had of teaching during your doctorate, any training you had for that role, and whether you have started to compile a teaching portfolio (Morss and Murray 2005), whether you have joined the relevant professional body, and so on.

Whether these more personal questions are about getting to know you, as a representative of the next generation of researchers in your field, or whether they are simply further examples of 'warm-up' questions, you will have to have some appropriate answers ready. Again, it might be best to keep your answers light, neutral and brief, and if not that, then whatever you think appropriate. As for all the questions in this chapter, the point is not simply to think through these questions, examiners' purposes and your reactions to them, but to create different forms of this type of question to give to your 'mock examiners' to use in your practice sessions.

General questions

General questions can be deceptively simple: they appear to ask for a general level of response. However, they can be very tricky, as they are often the more theoretical, conceptual or abstract questions. Clearly, dealing with general questions requires practice. The key skill is to avoid answering all such questions in general terms only. Refer to your thesis. Be specific.

The general question can be an easy opener, just to get things started, or it can be a starter for a series of more detailed questions:

- How did you come to be doing research in this area? Tell us a bit about how you came to do research in this area.
- Would you please summarize your thesis for us? Could you first summarize the main points of your thesis?
- You cover several areas in your thesis. What is the whole thing about?
- Who would you say are the key people in your field today?
- Did your study turn out as you expected?
- How do you see research developing in the next five years?

- On a general level, what, for you, were the most interesting things to come out of your thesis?

Do not feel bound to keep your answer general; go into some detail on some feature. Otherwise, your answers might be just too general. You might get a bit lost in abstraction. You might seem a bit vague. A discussion that remains at the general level too long might seem to lack substance. The examiner might start to wonder if you really know the work well. On the other hand, if the discussion is highly theoretical or conceptual, you will have to define your terms carefully, but you can still strengthen your answer with an example from your study and references to work you did and to others' work. You can – and some would say should – refer to your thesis in every answer.

Specific questions

These are often seen as the most difficult, since they are most focused on the study and less open to a range of answers. However, some students find them easier, in the sense that they focus the mind on material that is covered in the thesis and therefore help the candidate to locate an answer in the work done.

As the discussion moves on, the questions may focus on each phase of the research, from defining research questions and aims to methods, and so on. The discussion may progress through each chapter, starting with general questions and moving towards specifics. These may be questions that you have already answered in your chapters:

Questions the literature review should answer

- Why is this subject important?
- Who else thinks it is important?
- Who has worked on this subject before?
- What had not been done before?
- Who has done something similar to what you did?
- What did you adapt for your study?
- What is your contribution to the field?
- Who will use your material?

As you move to consider more specific questions it has to be emphasized that you are responsible for checking whether or not they are appropriate. Are these types of question asked in doctoral examinations in your discipline?

For students doing professional doctorates – are all of these questions relevant? Will there be more emphasis on questions related to professional or practice settings? Will there be less emphasis on empirical work and knowledge of the literature? Will examiners want to check your awareness of the role of research in practice settings? For example, the growing importance of research for school teachers might be a talking point in the examination of a professional doctorate in Education. Will examiners be more interested in your role as potential change agent, rather than independent researcher? Are these terms – or others – used on the report form that examiners use at your examination?

Whether or not you see these questions as relevant, whatever type of doctorate you are doing, you can always check. I have had conflicting feedback from students and examiners who attend my workshops and have read drafts of this book.

Some argue that these questions are relevant to all disciplines; some insist that these questions are only relevant to the humanities, while others argue that they are only relevant to the sciences.

The implications of these notes for all students are that they have to adapt these questions to suit their studies, and students on professional doctorates have to check which questions are relevant to their examination.

For similarly semi-specific questions, consult the *Handbook for External Examiners in Higher Education* (Partington et al. 1993: 76–7). Still focusing on the literature review:

- To what extent is the review relevant to the research study?
- Has the candidate slipped into 'here is all I know about X'?
- Is there evidence of critical appraisal of other work, or is the review just descriptive?
- How well has the candidate mastered the technical or theoretical literature?
- Does the candidate make explicit the links between the review and his or her design of the study?
- Is there a summary of the essential features of other work as it relates to this study?

Questions about other chapters or stages in the thesis are also provided. These questions are intended to guide external examiners in reading theses, but they may also help students to anticipate questions. Partington et al.'s handbook is not widely available, and students may find it useful to consult Pearce (2005) and Trafford and Leshem (2008), who provide lists of questions that have been asked in vivas.

Alternatively, or in addition, there may be questions about the relationship between your chapters, about your rationale or about your decisions:

- What is the link between your research questions and your hypothesis?
- Why did you reject other methods?
- What are the pros and cons of the methods you chose?
- Why did you reject the others?

It is impossible to predict how the examiner will use general and specific questions. For some, general questions will simply be used, perhaps spontaneously, as prompts for more specific discussions. Whatever the examiner's intention in asking such questions, it is worth remembering that you can decide to give long and detailed answers to both general and specific questions, thus demonstrating your knowledge. If the examiner wants you to give briefer answers, he or she will interrupt you or find some other way to tell you. You can, in other words, take a more active role in shaping your answers than you might think. You cannot know what type of answer they are looking for. You can make sure that they see how much you know about – or as a result of – your study.

The examples of questions provided in this section can only be considered as semi-specific. Each student must write more specific questions to be used in practice sessions. You can, of course, use the general and semi-specific questions in this section as a starting point, adding terms specific to your study to each question. Otherwise, you risk not being completely prepared to use the language and concepts of your particular study in the give and take of the discussion.

Each candidate has to write their own set of questions, if they are to be specific to his or her own study.

Open questions

> The truly open-ended question allows the person being interviewed to select from among his or her full repertoire of possible responses.
>
> (Patton 1982: 170)

The purpose of the open question is probably to give the candidate freedom to respond in his or her own terms, minimizing the likelihood of predetermined responses. In fact, the underlying assumption may well be that there can be no predetermined responses, that research matters are very much open to question, debate or interpretation.

Examiners who use open questions may want to find out what you think, not what you think about what they think. For example, the question 'What is your opinion of the work of X?' gives no cue as to how the examiner expects you to answer. Likewise, 'What did you think when you got that result/outcome of your experiment/analysis?' suggests that you have to frame your own answer, choose your own direction and select your own words. This can be quite demanding or liberating, depending on your attitude and aptitude.

Having said that, the examiner may suggest lines of answer, suggesting options for you to consider in your answer. Whether you will see these as being offered to you as explicit response alternatives or simply as potential debating points is worth thinking about in advance.

Those who have studied open and closed questions as part of their research methodology will be well ahead of the game here, but it might be as well to consider how your knowledge transfers to the context of your examination in practice and in some detail.

Closed questions

This is where there is clearly a set of fixed answers. The examiner might ask you whether researcher A used method X or Y. Clearly, you have to make a choice and, just as clearly, you have to be sure that your answer is the right one. If, on the other hand, you give an answer that you are told is wrong, or that you later, during the discussion, realize is wrong, then you can correct it. You might even want to explain your wrong answer: nerves, anxiety, a popular misconception, temporary memory loss, confusion.

The examiner might also be seeking information: 'What do you know about the work of X?' There might be a string of such questions, designed to test your knowledge of the detail of research methods, approaches or perspectives, for example.

Summarizing

We all know what summarizing means; what you do not know is how long the examiner would like your summary to be, if, that is, he or she has explicitly asked you for a summary. An important skill is to be able to summarize concisely the main points and to insert telling details at each point, combining the generalizations that are typical of summaries with specifics where possible and appropriate. The examiner may or may not state precisely what level of detail he or she is asking for. It may be up to you to decide what 'summarize' means.

Summarizing is deceptively simple, but it is easy to get bogged down in one part of the summary, to go into too much detail at the start and to fail to cover the whole subject. Summary, in general, requires us to be general.

Easy questions

For any thesis there will be easy questions, questions that are relatively straightforward, about subjects that are uncontested. Every student should anticipate what these questions might be. For every student what constitutes an easy question will be potentially different, depending on the nature of the work, perhaps. Writing down a few easy questions provides material for a less daunting early practice session. Naturally, this should be followed by a session with hard questions.

Hard questions

> This was the sort of question I disliked. There were so many things one could do my thoughts jostled into each other like a rugger scrum and became confused and unidentifiable.
>
> (Gordon 1952: 171)

For all students there is a question that they dread. This might be because they are less sure about an area of their work or because they perceive the examiner to be so knowledgeable in this area that their answer is bound to seem inadequate. Whatever the nature or the level of 'difficulty' presented by such questions, it is crucial, again, to write down two or three of your difficult questions and to practise answering them. Do not expect to be satisfied with your first practice answers; repeat the practice until you feel happier with your answer.

Writing down both an easy and a difficult question, then immediately practising them with other students, has proved a successful practical dimension to viva workshops. Students who do not have access to such workshops can still do this practice with peers, colleagues and friends.

Long questions

Sometimes questions are so long that you are not sure exactly what is being asked. This sometimes happens in the question-and-answer sessions after conference presentations, when someone is not really asking a question but giving a 'mini-paper'.

In your oral examination make sure that you understand what is being asked of you. You can, of course, always clarify or check with the examiner what he or she is asking, but you would not want to do that too often. You will not appear very competent if you have to keep asking, 'What is the question?'

Instead, you may have to take the initiative and tackle what you see as part of the question, at least. If you have been taking notes as the examiner asks his or her long question, then you may be able to work out what the question is on paper. Sometimes, however, the long question is just a long statement with a question tacked on at the end, so it is important to listen carefully right to the end. This is difficult to do if your anxiety levels are mounting with every word the examiner says. Again, this is where note taking may help; it gives you something to do, and you can use your notes to sketch your answer. Dealing with long questions, and actually answering them, is clearly another skill to practise well before your examination.

The 'second chance' question

If you give a poor answer to a question, you may find that you are asked it again, or asked to discuss the subject again in a different way. The examiner is not, therefore, necessarily trying to embarrass you by highlighting your mistake; instead, he or she may be giving you a second chance.

Examiners are likely to ask you a series of possibly quite closely related questions about the important areas of your work. Examiners may even appear to repeat themselves. However, it may be that they are seeking more specific answers than have been given to other questions. In other words, they may appear to ask the same question twice, or more than twice, in order to get at more detail. Examiners will not say, 'This is your second chance question', but they may find a way to come back to a point you covered earlier in the discussion using these – and other – techniques.

Methodological questions

The *Handbook for External Examiners in Higher Education* (Partington et al. 1993: 76–7) lists generic questions that, it is argued, are likely to come up, in some form, in vivas across the disciplines:

Questions about your methodology

• What precautions were taken against likely sources of bias?
• What are the limitations in the design? Is the candidate aware of them?

- Is the methodology for data collection appropriate?
- Are the techniques used for analysis appropriate?
- In the circumstances, has the best design been chosen?
- Has the candidate given an adequate justification for the design used?

It is, of course, possible to make such generic questions specific to your study:

- Summarize the steps in your research by condensing them into a series of sentences: 'The first step was . . . Then . . . The final step was . . .'
- Use the word 'step' – or some other word – to organize your answer.
- But what if they do not use the word 'steps'?
- This is why it is a good idea to practise more than once, with more than one type of question and more than one way of asking it. Then you have practised more than one way of answering the question.

See Trafford and Leshem (2002b: 41; 2008) for recurring questions about methodology in doctoral examinations:

- What led you to select these models of . . . ?
- What are the theoretical components of your framework?
- How did you decide upon the variables to include in your conceptual framework?
- How did concepts assist you to visualize and explain what you intended to investigate?
- How did you use your conceptual framework to design your research and analyse your findings?

There may be questions about what you did not do, requiring you to revisit early decisions. You should have some 'set pieces' on methodology, sequences of talk that you are comfortable giving, addressing these – or other – questions in these – and other – forms.

As you think about these questions it might help you to assume a position of superiority over your earlier self; you know so much more now than you did at the start of your doctorate. You should still argue for the quality of your data or analysis, of course, but you can also critique it. Score some points by naming other researchers who have done similar work. Show the examiner how well you know this other work and other methodologies. Examiners will be anxious to see that you are not too narrowly focused – and educated – in methodology.

Questions of methodology may, in some disciplines, be more about testing the framework within which you conducted your analysis or critique. If you had no more than a partially developed framework at the time of writing, you will have to make your analytical methods more explicit in the examination discussion (if you are asked to do so). However, remember, again, to start with what you did and to review what seemed like perfectly good reasons for doing so at the time, before you go on to critique your work or your writing in the light of your more recent understanding. You may, for example, have confused research design and research procedures, and you can demonstrate your new knowledge by teasing out the two during the examination. This is not to say that you should present your work as 'confusing'; if the examiner does not represent it as such, then you can, of course, represent it somewhere on the adequate–excellent continuum, in the same terms you used to define and defend it in your thesis argument.

Finally, you may not have provided sufficient critique of your chosen methodology in your chapter(s). Whether or not you have done this well, or at all, the examiner may prompt you to critique your methods during the oral examination. This is not to say that he or she is trying to find weaknesses; instead, the intention is to prompt you to rehearse the pros and cons of your method, with what might be, for you, a new emphasis on the latter. The purpose is not to expose the weaknesses in your work but to test the depth of your current understanding.

Questions about your writing

Each chapter of your thesis could produce questions for your oral examination, prompting you to revisit some of the decisions you made while writing it. Talk about writing as a series of achievements, a series of mini-closures, each teaching you something about your work and/or documenting something important. Make the story of the writing a coherent sequence of writing decisions and moments. Reveal how you acted on your supervisor's feedback on your writing. Clearly, you will be talking about your research in this way; it might be sensible to think of representing your writing in the same way.

Show that you understand that academic writing is a process, involving careful design, dialogue, feedback, conventions and many, many, many revisions. Reveal how you managed the series of steps in this complex process. The idea is to give the impression that you have learned how to manage this process and would be able to do so again, without supervision.

If you have publications, you can introduce these into the discussion. You can comment on the peer review you received. If you have submissions in the pipeline, mention them too. While the examination is primarily focused on your thesis, you should not feel that you cannot talk about other writing, particularly as publications signal the quality and impact of your work.

You may also have learned *through* writing. If so, do not be afraid to say so, as long as you can define what you mean and, to make your point clear, give an example.

While questions about writing might not seem as significant as questions about research, candidates should note that there is evidence that certain questions about the written text recur, and that core considerations should be included in students' preparation for this examination:

- Is the text of your thesis sufficiently transparent, with a perfectly clear intended meaning?
- Where will your readers see and recognize the doctoral worthiness of your thesis?
- How have you presented developing themes and issues so that examiners do not overlook or misunderstand the more complex aspects of your thesis?
- How will readers recognize the scholarly base upon which your text has been written? (Trafford and Leshem 2002b: 39)

There may also be questions that seem to be about the text of your argument but are actually about your research methods. For example, there may be questions about the match between data or analysis and conclusions: do your conclusions derive from, or are they supported by, your data or analysis? Ultimately, it might be difficult to separate research decisions and writing decisions. The key is to answer the examiner's question, using, if possible, the terms in which the question was asked.

Very specific questions may focus on exactly what you said on page X and exactly what you mean by that. The challenge is to remember what you meant or, if you cannot, to articulate what you seem to be saying, while disguising your lack of understanding of your own writing. On the other hand, it is probable that at some point in your thesis you have stated something unclearly, overstated a point or started a mini-argument that you then failed to develop sufficiently. The examination may in these cases be an opportunity to correct what you wrote some time ago or to develop more fully something that you wrote. You may want to use this as an opportunity to make a helpful connection with some other part of the thesis where your point is more developed. Finally, it is always possible that you would prefer to delete rather than develop a point you made in your thesis, but even then you should be clear about why and where you would do so. You do not want to get into too much editing and cutting, however, as your task at the oral examination is to make the case for what you wrote in your thesis, even if doing so is difficult.

Probing

A pattern in oral examination questions is variations on 'Why?' and 'Why not?' The examiner aims not only to check your thinking but also to establish that you checked it yourself. Even though you have thoroughly covered all that ground in your thesis, you have to revisit it and cover it just as thoroughly in your examination answers.

There are questions that probe for the compromises you were forced to make to your research design in your research procedures, such as 'To what extent did you feel that you had got all you needed by that point . . . or did you feel limited by time?' This question is not intended to force you to reveal weaknesses in the study, but is aimed at testing your understanding of what does and does not constitute a legitimate compromise, a compromise that still adheres to the standards required for doctoral research.

Aggressive questions

On the day itself I knew I was going to fail the moment I walked in. The questioning was off the topic and aggressive. One examiner tried to do his best to throw some straightforward questions my way, but it was clear they were not happy.

(Wakeford 2002: 35)

There are several reasons why examiners might be aggressive:

1 They might have an aggressive speaking style.
2 They might be anxious, excited, impatient, nervous or tense.
3 They may see it as appropriate behaviour, to see if you can cope with this style of questioning.
4 They may feel insecure, if they are new to the role or worried about relations with senior colleagues.
5 They may have concerns about your thesis (although this is no excuse for aggressive behaviour).
6 They may simply choose to 'grill' you, to put you under pressure, as, let us hope, for a minority of examiners, your examination is an opportunity for them to display their power.

Clearly, Wakeford's (2002) research shows that there is such a thing as bad behaviour by examiners, although we do not have enough detail on the event outlined in his article, nor do we have both sides of the story, a limitation of research based on reported experiences. However, his material should give us food for thought about what is and is not appropriate behaviour for examiners, particularly as bad experiences can have long-term effects for the students:

I found the whole experience of the viva extremely distressing and undermining: in fact nearly three years later I still think of it as a nightmare. I know I was there to defend my work, but I really felt under attack. One of the examiners in particular stated that the work had no proper theoretical base, and that the research was flawed. She criticized just about every aspect of the work that she could do. I knew sitting there that I had failed miserably, and that there would be at least another year or more of work to do, assuming I would be able to resubmit. My world felt like it was falling apart.

(Loumansky and Jackson 2004: 30)

This student was shocked to find that she has passed. While it is not appropriate to critique this student's responses, this example does raise the question, for those preparing for doctoral examinations to consider, of the distinction between probing critique – which is right – and undermining – which is wrong. In the context of the examination of your thesis, what would distinguish critical from undermining questions?

You just have to put up with it, some would say. Others would argue that you need to give as good as you get. A third way is to continue, at all times, to behave professionally, regardless of how the examiner behaves.

Follow-up questions

Any thesis will have core sections or issues that examiners will want to explore from a number of angles or perspectives. This is normal, and it can be interesting. It does not necessarily mean that the examiners are concerned about something; on the contrary, it will mean that they focus on a key area. This is often the area that they expect you to develop in future publications. If, however, you feel that their 'key area' is not what you consider the 'key area' of your research and your thesis, then you might want to consider and practise ways of redirecting the discussion.

The examiner may move towards a follow-up question by reflecting back what you have said. This sometimes sounds, to candidates, like a challenge, as if the examiner is really asking, 'Did you really mean to say that?' What they are actually saying is, 'So, what you are saying is . . .', to which the answer is yes, but you can also use this as an invitation or opportunity to extend your answer, and this may be its intention. If it is not, the examiner will probably ask you to move on.

Sometimes a follow-up question is designed to give the candidate a chance to clarify what he or she has said. Or it may be that you have a chance to develop more detail, to be more specific. If the examiner's response to your answer is silence, you might want to take this as a cue to continue developing your answer, to provide even more detail than you initially thought was required, drawing on and referring to your thesis.

This process might happen quite spontaneously: the examiner may not have a plan or schedule of follow-up questions. Instead, follow-up questions may be based on your answers. It might, therefore, be worth practising having someone ask follow-up questions that are 'taken', so to speak, from your answers. It is important to have some experience of that moment when you think you have given a sufficiently full answer, but back come two or three more questions, when you feel that you have answered the examiner's question, but back comes no feedback, only silence. You cannot allow yourself to be thrown by such moments, and you will not be if you practise.

Combined questions

Not all questions will be simple, in the sense that they have one part. Many questions will be complex, with two or more parts, and two or more questions within questions. For example, the examiner might ask a question like 'Can you summarize how your use of this method might lead to . . .?' In this question what appears to be a summary question is actually about cause and effect. It is important to remind yourself – before you attempt to answer – that you have already shown this in your thesis, or perhaps could develop it in order to project beyond your own work, clearly distinguishing the two as you speak. Your thesis is the examiner's starting point – for questions – and yours – for answers.

Answering this specific combined question is complex. A summary alone will not do. But it is important to make sure that you do give the summary part. Do not move straight to the apparently more complex aspect of the question until you have done the groundwork and 'scored some points' by demonstrating the rigour of your thinking and the soundness of your judgements. Take time to define your terms. Illustrate your points. Then, finally, move on to the part of the question about where this work will 'lead'.

Obvious questions

If you feel the questions are too superficial, if you feel you are stating the obvious, you can still develop in-depth answers. Treat simple questions with respect. Give a full answer. If you feel you must, give a fuller answer than the examiner appears to be looking for.

Remember that since you know your own work – and the work of others – so well, what seems obvious to you could still be a testing question, testing that you are in fact as knowledgeable as your thesis suggests. Rest assured that questions about first principles – whatever that means in your discipline – will be asked not in order to insult your intelligence but to test your understanding of the basics on which your study was founded.

However, if you feel you are not doing yourself justice because the questions are not getting to the 'meat' of your study, it is up to you to find a way to insert the highlights of your work. This is not to say that you should ignore a question that you feel is limited, but to say that you should link it to your work, talk about your work in depth and conclude by explicitly answering the question.

Hobby horses

If you look up 'hobby horse' in the dictionary you will find several definitions that I do not intend for this section. Instead, the term is used here to indicate that some examiners have their favourite questions, their favourite doctoral examination rituals and their favourite topics for examination discussions. You can see the sense in this: if the questions are tried and tested, if they stimulate discussion and enable the candidate to develop answers, then the examiner is likely to consider them effective and to use them again.

In addition, examiners' own ideas, preoccupations and ways of thinking inevitably shape how they play their role in your examination. Some examiners will try to be neutral, to keep their hobby horses under control, but others will let them run free. They might be quite open-minded, creative, interested to see where their hobby horse takes *you*. They may be curious to see whether or not you can bring the hobby horse into the corral.

You may, of course, have developed hobby horses of your own, but the viva is perhaps not the place to parade them.

The 'blue skies' question

What are the 'blue skies' questions? These are the exploratory, open-ended questions that are not necessarily tied to current research principles or programmes, or necessarily intended to produce fixed outcomes. What might this mean in terms of your project?

The '500,000 dollar' question

One examiner told me that he asked all his examinees the following question: if you had 500,000 dollars, euros, pounds, or whatever, to spend on your research, what would you do? The idea behind this question is, of course, to stimulate the candidate to speculate beyond the confines of his or her research while showing an understanding of: (1) what should be done next; (2) what could be done for that sum of money; and (3) how, exactly or approximately, it would be spent. On the one hand, this is a variation on the 'Where do you see research going in the next ten years?' question; on the other hand, it appears to require a much more focused and more specific answer.

In some disciplines students will have developed a good understanding of how research is costed; in others, less so. Every student must have a general idea of how research in their area should progress – in more than one potential direction – and perhaps that general idea should be developed slightly more specifically in order to prepare for this type of discussion. Simply having a general idea might not be enough.

In addition, the examiner might also be trying to gauge whether you have a realistic sense of what research involves and of how you might design a research process without supervision. In other words, this is a test of the doctoral criterion of 'Can the candidate do research independently?' Whatever the intention or form of the question, it would be good to have both general and specific answers. These should ideally be mini-arguments rather than a 'shopping list' of proposal statements about what 'should' be done. A mini-proposal would include the rationale for the proposed study (why does it need to be done?), aims of the study, methods to be used, feasibility, outcomes or deliverables, anticipating counter-arguments, etc. You can practise giving this type of answer, thinking about brief two-minute or more developed five-minute versions.

Repackaging questions

This is *not* to say that you should revise the examiner's questions during the examination, but for practice sessions you should consider the different ways in which a question might be asked or a topic might be raised. In this way, you are less likely to be taken aback by a question being asked differently from how you expected and practised it.

For example, the examiner might ask you to give an account of your contribution in different ways:

- Explain what is new about your work.
- Tell me how your work differs from that of X.
- When did you realize that you were on to something?
- What would you say has been your contribution?
- Who would be most likely to agree with you?
- Who would be most likely to disagree?

- How long do you expect your work to remain innovative?
- Do you think your research will influence others?

For such an important criterion, the examiner may use several questions or prompts.

All students must prepare an answer to the 'contribution' question; it is equally important that they do not wait until they are asked the question explicitly, but use the word at some point in more than one of their answers.

Understanding the question

Under pressure some people find that they have difficulty even understanding what is being asked, let alone what type of question is being used. This may be because we are so locked into our own way of thinking about our work that when someone asks us about it from their frame of reference it seems – momentarily at least – to make no sense. This is another reason to practise with someone who will ask you questions in different forms. You can learn to work through that moment of incomprehension.

It would probably be taking this point too far to try to anticipate how your examiner, once you know exactly who he or she is, will ask questions. Any examiner is likely to use more than one form of question in any case. On the other hand, you may be able, through discussion with others who have more experience of doctoral examinations in your discipline, to identify recurring questions. Again, it would be smart to practise using these and to ask the people you are practising with to vary the form of the question.

If, during your oral examination, you find that you do not understand the question, you can always say so and ask the examiner to repeat it, but you probably do not want to do that too often. Writing the question down – see 'Taking notes' in the next chapter – is one way of focusing your attention on what exactly is being asked. Your notes can also trigger potential answers.

Listening

In order to understand the questions you have to listen. You may also want to use non-verbal behaviours, such as nodding, to show that you are listening carefully. As the examiner is speaking, you have to focus. Exactly what is he or she asking you about? What exactly is the question? A key focusing strategy for yourself is to ask yourself the question, how does that relate to my work and my thesis? If you can pick out and write down the key words in the examiner's questions you have a method of ensuring that you use them in your answers.

'Doctorateness'

What guidelines have you used to draft your research proposal so that prevailing notions of doctorateness are reflected in an explicit manner? How have you displayed doctorateness in an overt manner within your thesis?

(Trafford and Leshem 2002b: 37)

While 'doctorateness' might seem an odd – even new – word for some students, examiners and supervisors, its use here does pose a particular type of question, inviting students to consider, explicitly, where in the thesis they have engaged, explicitly, with doctoral criteria.

Facets of 'doctorateness' include research design, presentation, coherent argument, quality of writing, a kind of three-way 'fit' of design, outcomes and conclusions and initial and final contextualization. If there are other characteristics of doctorateness at your institution or in your discipline, then you should be ready to indicate where you evidence these in your thesis and then demonstrate them in your discussion ability.

Whether or not you think you need to talk about general, or other, local doctoral criteria, it is generally agreed that one criterion is an essential subject for discussion in doctoral examinations, originality.

The originality question

- What is original about your work?
- What sets your work apart from others'?
- What do you think you produced that was really new?

Be ready for this question, in a range of forms. You will have dealt with this question somewhere in the thesis, so start with the points you made there. You now have to debate the points you made in your thesis orally in your examination.

In addition, you might, in hindsight, want to claim more or less than you did in the introduction or conclusion to your thesis. Your work may have been confirmed or challenged by more recent publications. Show that you have read these and understand how they relate to your work.

If the word 'originality' does not come up, it is up to you to make sure it is mentioned, debated or at the very least perceived.

'Is there anything you'd like to ask us?'

After examiners have finished asking their questions, they usually have a final question: do you have any questions for us? There are several typical questions to consider:

- Follow up on earlier stages in the discussion by asking if you can elaborate on an earlier answer in order to develop your point further.
- Ask the examiner for a view on potential publications in the thesis.
- If you feel that you have not covered an important topic at all, or in sufficient depth to do it justice, ask if you can discuss it now.
- If you think you made an error earlier, or gave a weak answer, ask if you can correct, or develop, it now.

Each of these questions leads in a different direction, and it is acceptable to ask more than one question or more than one type of question.

Note that the focus at this stage of the discussion is still your thesis. This is not an opportunity to ask the examiner what he or she thinks about your performance or to ask what the outcome is. This is a chance to obtain valuable advice on the potential for future publications.

Your 'set' of questions

Students and supervisors can use the collection of questions in this chapter to put together a likely 'set' of questions that: (1) are likely to come up; and (2) the student can use or adapt in order to prepare to discuss well. In such a 'set' there is likely to be a mixture of different types of questions.

Make up your own set of questions

- How important were ethical considerations in your study?
- How did you handle them?
- Were there no safety issues? For participants? For yourself?
- How did you resolve these?
- Who do you think will be influenced by your work?
- How do you think that influence will occur?

- How did you develop the . . . you used in your methodology?
- Did you use the same technique with each subject/material?
- What do you mean when you use the term . . . ?
- Did you consider how you might have to curtail a phase of your research, if you saw that it was not working?
- Why should we trust the analysis you present in Table X?
- Why was . . . a good judgement?
- Why should we accept your interpretation of . . . ?
- Which is your most important recommendation and why?
- Do you think your recommendations are feasible?
- You say . . . was the result of . . . Could it have been the opposite?
- You seem unsure of . . . Why is that?

Discussion in doctoral examinations should be of the highest standard and should not be left to chance. It is not adequate for an examiner to say to a pre-examination student, 'Well, let's just wait and see . . . You've nothing to worry about . . . I'm sure you'll be fine.' Nor is it adequate to say, 'Murray's/Partington et al.'s/Trafford's questions are completely irrelevant in our discipline', unless, of course, the speaker goes on to provide alternative questions for students to use in their practice sessions.

Finally, as you develop your 'set' of questions, watch out for symptoms of 'doctoral myopia', a hypothetical condition that prevents you from seeing – or getting – outside of your 'box'. If you are the only person preparing practice questions, you are likely to be limited in your range. The cure is to incorporate other perspectives. Check your set of questions with someone else. Increase the range by asking others to develop questions for you. Do not automatically exclude from your practice sessions questions that take you by surprise or seem too far off the subject. Exclude some, but keep a few. While you do not want to be drawn too far from your thesis, in the examination discussions, such questions are useful for making you do the hard work of creating a link between the question and the thesis. This is an art in itself.

The tactic of using the thesis as a starting point in the development of answers is dealt with, along with many other strategies for answering questions in the doctoral examination, in the next chapter.

Checklist

- PhD, professional doctorates and PhD by publications – each will have specific requirements and criteria for the oral examination. Students can use the generic questions provided in this chapter and adapt them to suit their theses and their types of doctorate.

- This means literally writing out a range of different types of question. These can then be used in practice sessions outlined in Chapter 8.
- Some would argue that the approach adopted in this chapter (and throughout this book) – that students can and should take the initiative in preparing for the examinations – takes no account of the culture of inequality operating in universities, as in other institutions:

> The current climate of lifelong learning in the academy suggests that students should take responsibility for their own learning. Such individualism enables advice to research students to continue to be that it is for them to face the horrors of the viva and try to deal with them (Murray, 2003[b]). Such advice takes no heed of patterns of inequality, nor does it call institutions to account.
>
> (Loumansky and Jackson 2004: 31)

I take the point that 'patterns of inequality' do exist and operate to keep power in a limited number of hands. I also accept the criticism that my writing does not 'call institutions to account'. However, I would respond by saying that it is precisely because of the potential for undermining, disempowerment and abuse that I set out to support students preparing for their examinations. Throughout this book, there are references to – rather than critiques of – power dynamics in the doctoral examination, but my purpose is to help students to cope with them. I would still maintain that students need to be active in their preparations, while involving others in their practice sessions. Some of these issues are taken up in the next chapter.

6

Answers

On the day of the examination, a certain level, and perhaps type, of performance will be required. The characteristics of strong and weak performances – and the reasons for them – are outlined in detail in this chapter. While the strategies proposed here will be challenged by some, the question is whether such challenges are prompted by the strategies themselves or by the very notion that something that they see as unique and obscure could be 'reduced' to a set of strategies. This chapter is, therefore, in itself challenging, since it begins to reveal aspects of the doctoral examination that are usually completely unspoken. This might present problems for students who want to discuss the topic of examination answers with supervisors who have not considered this level of detail. However, as a growing body of evidence, referred to throughout this and the previous chapter, trickles down through the system it should become more common knowledge and, ultimately, common practice.

For students, there are reminders throughout this book for you to check current practices in your own institution. However, while the oral examination is very individualistic – each examination is different – there are certain behaviours that you ought to consider and, if appropriate, practise well in advance. Definitions and examples of these are provided.

Check your institution

- You ought to get yourself to a position where you can 'read' the context in which your examination is likely to take place and to consider what 'performing well' means in your department or discipline.
- It is up to you to research what constitutes effective answers in your department, perhaps also in your discipline and perhaps even for your external examiner.
- Given the documented wide variation in doctoral examination practices across and within institutions, this can be a mini-research project in its own right.

Examiners and supervisors will have their own views on what constitutes good practice in answers and you should do whatever you can to find out what that is. Some will have thought it through more than others, of course, and there is no need to stick with the level of your supervisor's definition of good practice.

In order to address the needs and contexts of a wide range of students, a wide range of answering strategies is covered in this chapter, some providing direct answers to typical doctoral examination questions, others aiming to achieve some other goal simultaneously. For example, students do not just provide answers to questions, but also demonstrate their knowledge of their subjects.

If, as you read this chapter, you find that one particular type of answer does not seem appropriate for you, you might, of course, simply skip to the next one. Alternatively, you could produce an alternative answer – similar answer, different form for your discipline perhaps – and practise that.

It is not the intention of this chapter to represent the student as a passive recipient of whatever the examiners ask, following them wherever they choose to go with their questions. Instead, a case is made for a more active role for the student. There is evidence that students can influence the 'discursive process' in their oral examinations by using 'communicative strategies that are predictive and deliberative' (Trafford and Leshem 2002b: 37). This means going *beyond* simply checking the stated procedures in your institution. It means that simply demystifying the doctoral examination is not sufficient. It means that students have to understand the components of communicative strategies, to customize them for their own examinations and to practise them well in advance to the point where the strategies have become part of their own rhetorical repertoire. Such strategies may even prove to be useful beyond the examination. If this is to be achieved, students have to accept that they are in a learning process as they prepare for the examination; they are not just picking up hints and tips but taking their existing communicative strategies to a higher level.

New skills

In many respects the doctoral examination is a first: the candidate's first oral examination, the first full discussion of the completed thesis with another expert, the first time an independent reader has read the whole thesis carefully and, perhaps, the first time the whole text has been critiqued *as a whole*. For students this means that you have to consider how you can use your existing skills in new ways, raise your verbal skills to a higher level and, if need be, develop new skills. Exactly which new or improved skills you will have to develop may not become clear until you have begun to practise for your oral examination.

This means making explicit the questions you have *already* answered in your thesis (covered in the previous chapter). This can be easier said than done because it involves two processes – at least – that paradoxically might appear to be of a lower order of skill:

- recalling earlier decisions;
- making conscious your subconscious thought processes.

It could be precisely this paradox that prevents some doctoral students from seeing their way to preparing thoroughly for the examination. This could be the cause of some of the 'disasters' that we have all heard about: the student feels that he or she knows the subject so well that there is no need to do the basic revision steps of recall and reprocessing with sample questions. Such a student might even – understandably – be under the illusion that such basic forms of preparation are beneath the standard required for the doctorate.

Some of the strategies introduced in this chapter will be new to some candidates. In some ways the strategies are similar to the strategies we use in academic writing and, therefore, to strategies that you used in writing your thesis. The key new skill may be using such strategies in speech.

'Decorum'

Defining the decorum of the doctoral examination means determining the type of behaviour that is suitable or appropriate to this occasion. Is it the same as other discussions you have already had about your thesis? Or is the doctoral examination more like a job interview, requiring more formal behaviour? In fact, it could be argued that the doctoral examination is like a combination of examination – in aim – and interview – in form. The style of behaviour appropriate for this examination is, therefore, clearly formal, perhaps in the direction of respectful without being subservient.

To a certain extent, behaviour is a matter of personal style; there are no codes of conduct to guide students on exactly how to behave in this context. In fact, the very concept of this type of code of conduct would seem laughable to some. However, some examiners like the doctoral examination to be a bit of a ritual and will expect you to indicate by your behaviours that you take it very seriously indeed.

Annual reviews or upgrade interviews should have given you some idea of and practice in this scenario, but the presence of an external examiner is bound to affect the ambience. The best tactic might be to follow your examiner's lead: does he or she adopt a formal or informal tone? Alternatively, you can decide to remain formal and polite regardless of how he or she behaves.

Greetings and titles

At some point in the opening seconds of your examination the chair of the meeting should introduce everyone to you, even if you already know most of the people in the room quite well. These introductions are there for clarification and, sometimes, to put you at your ease.

Depending on how well everyone knows everyone else, the greetings may be formal or informal. They may use their titles or they may decide to use first names. In the latter case it is probably not a signal that you should do likewise, unless you are explicitly asked to do so.

As introductions are made, the examiner may be trying to gauge how tense or relaxed you are. Do not worry if you feel unable to hide your nerves. This is to be expected. Remember that in this type of situation most people look and sound less nervous than they feel. Besides, it will not surprise your examiner that you are nervous. In fact, the examiner might be surprised if you were not. It may even be a good thing not to appear too relaxed, in case you have drawn an examiner who likes to take confident candidates down a peg or two.

Talking about writing

Talking about your thesis, always the starting point, involves verbalizing a written argument, face-to-face with someone who is ready to come at you with the counter-arguments. This means that debate, dialogue and demonstration replace the contingent closure of the written word:

- debate points that you have already debated in your thesis;
- hold your ground while acknowledging refutations;
- participate in the give and take of different perspectives;
- use careful explanation to show that you know your subject.

The discussion is likely to be a more open, perhaps disrupted, set of arguments and 'texts'. The progression from one point to another will not necessarily follow the pattern of your thesis argument or expression. However, your answers should show some of the same continuity that you constructed in your writing, even if you now have some reservations about that. You should be able to do the following:

- construct narratives of the work you did;
- show the progression in and logic of your thinking;
- show connections;
- reveal how continuity and closure were constructed.

You can, of course, reveal any reservations you have about your work and discuss your more recent thinking, but be sure to do justice to what you have done before you start revising it.

It might be helpful, in preparing to answer questions about your written argument, to see it again as disaggregated. This may seem counter-intuitive, given that you invested so much time in inventing and refining its almost hermetically sealed logic, but the thesis is still a work of discourse, and it might help you to start seeing it that way again. The trick is to see your thesis in a completely new way:

- see your thesis as a series of questions and answers;
- think about it as a series of mini-arguments;
- list the assumptions on which it rests;
- identify assertions and speculations you have made;
- isolate references that appear throughout the thesis;
- list side issues and tangents that were not developed;
- separate out the different facets of the subject of your research;
- describe one or two units in your research separately from the others;
- break up linked 'sets' of aims and outcomes;
- break up your conclusions into parts;
- develop one as a mini-proposal.

As you break your thesis down, you should continue to make links as you talk, between parts of your work and between the sections of your writing. You may find that you have to make different types of links for different types of structure. Once you have practised this a few times, you will be ready for any type of question. You will be able to represent your work in several different ways.

At some point in the discussion, specific features of your written text are likely to be the focus of some questions, such as:

- On page 125 you say . . . What do/did you mean by that?
- Are you saying that . . .?
- Are you sure about that?

In this case, rather than trying to remember exactly what you meant on every single line, turn to page 125, restate what you have written, expand on that a little, or paraphrase it in different terms if you prefer, then answer the examiner's question. Restating will help you to recall what it is you were thinking about at the time of writing or revising. Paraphrasing will save you from simply repeating yourself and may help you to elaborate on the point. Both of these give you time to think about how you want to answer the question. The mechanics of this interaction, including physically turning to the exact page and making sure everyone is looking at the correct point on that page, might be worth practising.

Remember that even though you are discussing your own writing, and even though the thesis is now a fixed text, you are still engaged in discourse. You do not have to 'prove' that what you said then is right now. However, you do have to demonstrate that you had good reason for writing what you did, or, if you wish to revise it, that you do so in the light of deeper understanding and increased knowledge. Do not be too quick to change what you wrote; the examiner wants to check that you understand why you wrote it and even that you wrote it yourself. You should not treat every question about any word of your thesis as an invitation to revise your thesis.

Structuring answers

There are many recurring structures in academic arguments. You will have noted many of them in your reading, even if you have not used every single one in your writing:

- classification: groupings (e.g. of researchers, methods, etc.);
- analysis: breaking the subject into parts;
- pros and cons;
- problem–solution;
- general–specific;
- narrative (of work done);

- other directions/structures;
- the structure of your thesis argument.

Of these, perhaps pros and cons is one of the strongest, since it is your tool for showing that you can see – indeed, have seen for some time – that there is more than one side of the issue. You use this structure to signal explicitly that you are able to consider and articulate more than one set of methods appropriate for research on your chosen problem and more than one way of explaining the results of your research. You can, and perhaps should, use the words pros and cons explicitly, thus clearly labelling the directions in your thinking and your ability to conduct this debate.

You should be able – in speech – to integrate the parts of your thesis, the chapters and sections, the aims and outcomes and the stages in your research. If you do not do this, the examiner may not see the links. How often will the examiner have read your thesis? Once on a scan and once in detail? Or more often? Remember that you have to do some work orally to show how the coherence of your work and your writing fit. If integration is your aim, then 'integration' – or forms of the word – is the word you should use.

This may, again, involve you rehearsing arguments that you have made pretty thoroughly in your thesis. On the other hand, the examiner may propose something new and you may have to think on your feet about its pros and cons. However, there is no need to rush to answer: using the pros and cons structure gives you time to weigh things in the balance and to come up with a measured answer.

Verbal strategies

The skills of oral debate involve specific verbal strategies that may be quite particular to your discipline of study. You should discuss these with your supervisor(s): what constitute weak and strong strategies in debates in your discipline? One key weakness would be undeveloped answers, where the speaker for some reason assumes that details are not needed:

Weak strategies

- [The work is] useful.
- I suppose not.
- What do you think?
- That's about the size of it.
- All right.
- It's what happened.
- I don't know.

- If you put it that way.
- I made acknowledgements in everything I wrote.
- All the interpretations that I made were mine.
- No.
- I suppose so (Snow 1960: 217–21).

None of these answers is 'wrong' in itself; it is the fact that they are so short, so undeveloped, that is dangerous for the candidate. He or she has not given a reason for the answer, expecting the short answer to do all the work; nor has he or she shown the thinking behind the answer.

Many would judge this performance, if it were extended to the whole or a greater part of the examination, to be a failure, on the grounds that the candidate has not genuinely answered the questions: on the one hand, answers have, literally, been given; but, on the other hand, the minimal responses say nothing about how the answers were generated, how the candidate arrived at the answers. In other words, these poor responses emphasize that the *workings behind* the answers are as important as the answers themselves. None of these responses allow us to see the candidate's thinking ability. Perhaps more damagingly, some of these responses show a defensiveness that has clearly militated against the candidate taking the questions seriously.

These examples are taken from a work of fiction, C. P. Snow's novel *The Affair*, and they all appear in the story of one oral examination, the circumstances of which are, it is to be hoped, more strained than would normally be the case. However, for the purposes of this chapter they serve to illustrate the types of answers not to give, unless you are particularly concerned to be the most concise speaker in the room during your examination. Whether or not that is a sensible goal is a sensible question.

Starting with the thesis

Candidates who provide satisfactory responses to the predictable questions confirm the opinion of examiners towards doctoral level of the thesis . . . Candidates who do not address and provide satisfactory answers to the predictable questions in their thesis, will not be able to impress the examiners who gain their initial impression of the doctoral worthiness by their independent reading of that thesis.

(Trafford and Leshem 2002b: 47–8)

These researchers make a strong case for the thesis being not only the source of candidates' practice questions but also the reference point for their answers. It could be argued that any answer – to any question – could and perhaps should start with the thesis. The thesis is the record of the work done. In a sense, all the answers must be there. Certainly the starting point to all answers lies there.

Using your thesis as your starting point requires you to think about which part of the thesis is relevant to the examiner's question:

- Which chapter has anything to do with the question?
- Is there an answer to the question in any of the chapters?
- More than one chapter? Which one first?
- Summarize what happens in that chapter.
- Refer to and turn to specific pages.
- Say why it is relevant to the question asked.
- Check: have you answered the question?

If you have done your homework well, you will be able to direct discussion towards the highlights in your work on, for example, page 157. Where are the highlights: page 157 and where else? If you have not already done so, identify the pages that you want to ensure the examiner sees and discusses. Decide in advance which pages you want to highlight, including page 157. Once you have established that, as this paragraph shows, page 157 is a key page, it does not take a lot of memory work to remember it. It does, however, take practice to become skilled at directing discussion towards it. With practice you can easily move from a range of quite different questions to your selected highlight answers, comfortably citing specific pages as you go. Some people are brilliant at this, but there is no need to assume that it is a gift that you either have or do not have. It can be learned.

Similarly, choose two or three names (and dates) from the literature. Learn the titles and places of their key publications, particularly groundbreaking or 'corner turning' publications. Score points by giving this level of detail, not about every single researcher but about the key people. Then find a way to link them and your work. You have already written something of this type in your conclusions, but practise doing this verbally.

Choosing vocabulary

Remember not to overlook the standard vocabulary of research design and reporting:

- aims;
- objectives;
- analysis;
- theoretical framework.

Remember that simply having written about such terms is not enough; practise using them in discussion to the point where you are fluent and comfortable doing so.

Likewise, it is important to speak the language of your discipline fluently, to use specialist terms correctly and clearly and to make sure that you define how you are using them carefully. While all disciplines share their set of terms, there is often debate within disciplines about the precise meanings of terms. Do not worry if you are asked to explain 'what you mean by X', as this is a standard probe to find out whether you understand the particular – not the general – meaning of the term in relation to your research. Are you able and ready to discuss the possible meanings of key terms and to select the meaning most appropriate to your work? Some of this ground must have been covered in your thesis, unless the question of terminology was not at all relevant. You do not have to prepare better definitions than you already have in your thesis; instead, you have to make the case for the ones you used. You may benefit from practice in rehearsing these definitions orally.

Defining

It is up to you to demonstrate that you understand key terms, concepts and processes in your field. This is particularly true if you have invented terms yourself or adapted an established term to produce a new usage or meaning.

Perhaps more importantly, you may be using key, familiar or specialized terms in particular ways in your research and your speech. Make that clear: 'By X I mean . . .', 'I have used X to refer to . . .'. You may also want to point out how your use of the term compares with how other researchers in your field have used it. Examiners may act out debates about meanings of words you have used in your thesis: 'X does not have the same meaning for you as it does for me. Can you explain that?' This may feel like a challenge to the definition you have used, which it is. The first step in any answer should be to start with the definition provided in the thesis, recreating the argument for it. You can then compare available definitions, answering the question by acknowledging that there are different uses of the word for specific purposes that you can summarize.

Even though you and your examiner are both very knowledgeable in the area – you all know the key terms – you still have to show that you know them. It is up to you to demonstrate that you are fluent in key terms – and in their definitions – and comfortable using the full vocabulary of research in your field. Remember that what you might experience as embarrassment at explaining basic terms and concepts to experts they might mistake for discomfort or unfamiliarity with those terms.

Using definition carefully is one way of shifting your use of language into a more precise and exact style. You have to make clear what you are – and are not

– saying. There can be no fudging in this type of oral examination. In a sense, this requires you to bring some of the skill and precision that you normally use in writing to your speaking.

While definition is deceptively simple, many debates hang on the particular use of a word, or the appropriateness of one word to the argument that follows it. These debates are far from simple, but they are sometimes dismissed as petty or no more than 'semantics'. Whether or not you think it is all a matter of semantics, you do have to define your terms carefully. Juggling different definitions is an important intellectual skill evidenced in, for example, your discussion of the literature, of alternative methodologies or of your developing understanding. You may even have changed your use of a term in the course of your work. You may be using it in more than one way. You may realize now that this is a bit confusing or incoherent. Defining your terms in a discussion can make clear what you are saying and can stop you from apparently contradicting yourself. Since you have probably not had to do this with your supervisor for some time, it might be an idea to practise this.

Define-and-illustrate

Having defined the terms of your discussion, or of a specific answer, there can be no better follow-up than to illustrate your point. The combination of definition and illustration shows the reader or listener exactly what your point is. The listener may not agree with you but will see that you have a good point. If you can support your point with evidence, then so much the better, but illustration makes the point clear and that is a crucial step in any argument.

The define-and-illustrate strategy requires you to think about going into 'for example' gear regularly in your discussions. As you begin an answer, be sure that it is clear how you are using key terms – define them – and then move into second gear by illustrating the point. Where can you find illustrations for your points? In your thesis.

Define–defend

This is a key strategy for doctoral examinations. Students have found it useful in preventing them from becoming overly defensive in their answers. It also helps them to think their way into their role as candidates. The doctoral examination is – or should be – the scene of intense debate about a piece of completed work. It should be assumed that there will be disagreement and perhaps even a conflict of views.

For students, the temptation is to respond to challenging, probing questions with defence and justification of their work. This is understandable. However, a stronger strategy is to begin with a definition of the work – say *what* you did – and then, only then, say *why* you did it that way. Define first, defend second:

- *Examiner's question*. Why did you not do more detailed analysis of . . .?
- *Candidate's 'defend' answer*. I did not do that because . . .
- *Define–defend answer*. What I did was . . . My reasons for doing that were . . . I could have done a more detailed analysis of . . . by . . . But I decided not to do that because . . .

This strategy has the added advantage that it shifts the tone: instead of falling into a defensive pattern, the candidate rehearses decisions made during the research and documented in the thesis. It can also prevent candidates from actually becoming defensive. It allows the candidate to talk about the work and the thesis, and includes the important practices of explaining processes, narrating experiences and demonstrating knowledge.

Being specific

This might seem like an obvious point: if you want to demonstrate knowledge and to indicate that you did the work yourself, you have to be specific. However, as in all examinations, ambiguity surrounds the examiner. The examiner, it is posited, 'knows all the answers already'. The examinee thinks that there is no point in spelling out a point that the examiner already knows. As all successful exam takers know, the point is not to educate the examiners but to show them what you know.

Being specific in your speech means giving names, dates, places, frequency of occurrence and other indicators of detail appropriate to your discipline. If you do not have any of these names and numbers, you are probably not being specific. Your thesis will be riddled with specifics; there is no need to go out and find new ones.

Linking the general and the specific is a tactic for showing that you understand the importance of the specifics you select within the broader debate being conducted by researchers in your field. Following a general statement with a specific statement is a good strategy for building an argument, showing that you can support your view with evidence and/or reference to some other authority.

Think about what it would be sensible for you to be specific about. Where would it make most sense for you to be specific? Where can you manage at a more general level in your answers? For example, you will probably want to be

able to be specific about the key people in your field, to show that you know
their work particularly well:

- When did they publish their first key work?
- What was its title?
- Where was it published?
- What precisely did they say in their key paper or book?
- What contribution did they make?

Answering these questions may seem to you now as no more than a matter
of summarizing, but to do this well, you might want to revise the detail of,
say, three of the key people in your field, perhaps the ones who relate most
closely to your own work. Revise your literature review, or your use of the
literature in your thesis, by selecting specific details that you are comfortable
using in speech. Even choosing the top three people in your field might be a
complex task:

- Who was responsible for the major 'conceptual turns', innovations or
  significant changes in thinking in your field?
- What have these people published recently, including after you completed
  your thesis?

The highlights of your research – whatever you take them to be, or whatever
you want to argue that they are – might be another sensible set of topics for
specific talking on your part. This might also be a good way of re-engaging
with your thesis after being away from it for some time.

How specific is specific? How detailed do you need to be? You might want to
follow the non-verbal cues of your examiner: does he or she look like they
want you to continue? Or do they all look like they want to move on to a new
question? Do they want you to carry on developing your answer? Or do they
look satisfied with what you are saying? You can, of course, ask them if they
want you to continue, but if they are sitting looking attentive, then you can
continue talking. As always, if you do find yourself giving a long, detailed
answer, remember to answer the question you were asked.

Above all, do not feel that you have to wait until the examiner asks you to
'please be more specific'. Some examiners may indeed want to call all the
shots, but you should at least consider taking the initiative. If you do not speak
in specifics at some point you may give the impression that you do not have
sufficiently detailed knowledge. The knowledge you reveal may seem too
superficial for the doctoral level.

If you feel you are not being allowed to develop your point, if you feel you
are being shut down, what will you do? What can you do to make sure that you
do yourself justice? What can you do to make sure that the examiner sees the
specifics of your work?

Rather than quietly – or visibly – becoming frustrated, you can, of course, simply ask for a minute or two to be more specific: 'Would you mind if I took a minute or two to develop this point?'; 'I'd like to give an example of this from my thesis'; 'I can illustrate this point by . . .'; 'I feel I have not given a full answer to your question, although I have covered this area in Chapter . . . and I would like to discuss that briefly'; 'I give an example of this/a detailed explanation of this/an analysis of the pros and cons of this in Chapter . . . of my thesis, where I state that . . .'

If the examiner refuses to grant your request, once or twice, in order to move on to the next question, then you may feel that you have to follow his or her lead. If, however, the examiner refuses to let you do this at all, you may feel that you are being treated unfairly and will have to be ready to manage your emotions. You will also have to find a different way of introducing your specifics. If the examiner repeatedly cuts you off as you try to be specific, and if the decision made at the end of your examination is not good, you may have grounds for an appeal. This type of railroading behaviour does sometimes happen, often as the result of a competitive dynamic between examiners.

Being explicit

Being explicit presents a similar challenge to being specific: in any examination, some students think that the examiner will know what they mean, and that they therefore do not need to spell out explicitly what they mean. The examiner has, after all, read the thesis. It may seem artificial to spell out what the examiner has already read. However, one of the aims of the examination is to check that you did the work yourself and, if you have, this can only be revealed to the examiner in your more detailed discussions.

Some candidates will feel that they are insulting the examiner's intelligence by making explicit something the examiner is bound to know already. You may feel that your examiner knows much more than you and does not need explanations. This may, of course, be true, but remember that the purpose of this examination is not to educate them about your area, but to show that you have been educated in this area. It is your job to reveal this to the examiner.

You may have to be explicit in another sense: you may be asked to revisit decisions made during the research process. The examiner may be looking for more transparency in your thesis: for example, what was it about your findings that made you judge them to be sufficiently interesting to be considered *as* findings? This is one of the more demanding aspects of the doctoral examination. You have to reveal the mental processes behind decisions documented in the thesis. It might be a good idea to revisit some of these decisions before your examination. The thesis will not contain all the reasons for all your decisions; this is no reason to panic. Instead, it is a prompt to recall and to practise reworking some of the processes spontaneously, since it is impossible to predict all possible questions of this type.

To complicate matters further, you may recall that there were various influences on your analytical processes, including your desire to do something different from what others had done. In certain contexts, such subjectivity is not necessarily wrong: there is such a thing as claiming too much objectivity, i.e. more objectivity than is merited by the methods used. The thing to remember is that the examiner is likely to be more interested in the checking mechanisms you used to ensure that your analysis was sound. They may also be interested to see if you can critique your own checking mechanisms, in the light of what you now know. It is likely that you can, given that you are more knowledgeable about the subject and about research methods now than you were then. If you now know that your checking mechanisms could have been more robust, you can say so, but not until you have established the value of what you did. For each of these phases, on each of these points, it is important that you are as explicit in your discussions as you were in your writing and possibly even more so.

Elaborating

The word 'elaborate' means working through a topic minutely, painstakingly and in detail. It is important for demonstrating qualities like thorough searching, rigour in methodology and depth of understanding.

There is one school of thought that says that all your answers should be as concise as possible, that examiners will become impatient with long-drawn-out answers and will look upon candidates unfavourably as a result. However, another school of thought says that you should develop your answers, provide detail and consider pros and cons, an approach that makes for longer, more complex answers. This gives you a chance to do justice to your work. It prevents you from giving answers that are too general. It might make you appear more able to be critical of your work, and in your thinking generally, if, for example, you demonstrate an ability to see more than one side of an issue.

In any case, is it possible to judge what constitutes 'enough' elaboration? Is it not a good strategy to continue elaborating until the examiner appears to be ready to ask the next question? Or should you assume that since you might not be able to judge accurately when the examiner does, and does not, want to move on, it might be sensible for you to keep talking until you are interrupted? This approach gives you some control over how the time is used and ensures that you answer some questions in detail.

There is nothing wrong with taking the initiative in this way. In practice, you may have no indication of how detailed or general an answer the examiner is looking for, so it might be better to err on the side of detail, at least some of the time, and give fuller answers and use elaboration to bring in the detail of your thesis and your thinking.

This might take practice, since it involves you making links between the general and the specific, between different questions and the detail you want to introduce into the discussion, as you talk, perhaps making new connections between aspects of your research and writing. Speaking at length and choosing the direction of elaboration might not be something you have done recently or regularly, and is therefore a skill to practise in advance of the examination.

Speaking in the past tense

There is no need to speak in one tense throughout the discussion, but speaking in the past tense means that you talk about your work as a *completed* project, about your findings as having been *interpreted* in a certain way, for certain reasons, and about your conclusions as an argument *constructed* at a certain point in time, in the past. By contrast, when you use the present, or continuous present, tense, you risk giving the impression that you claim universal relevance or meaning for your work.

The difference between the two is clearer when we consider examples:

Why use the past tense?

- To give an account of work done, e.g. 'What I did was . . .'.
- To explain decisions made earlier, e.g. 'I did that because . . .'.
- To reveal what you learned, e.g. 'I thought then that [explanation] . . . I now think . . .'.
- To avoid claiming universality, e.g. 'What this meant was . . .'.
- To demonstrate that you are reflexive about the learning process, e.g. 'What I learned from this was . . .'.

'What this means' implies that the interpretation has current, perhaps general, validity, whereas 'What this meant', or 'What I took this to mean' refers to an interpretation made and clearly situated in the past. This is an important point: you are demonstrating that you perceive your thesis not as an end in itself but as a contribution to an ongoing debate and/or programme of work.

Decisions you made during the project and while writing the thesis cannot be changed during the examination; you can and should represent them as sound and justifiable, given your knowledge or perspective at the time of writing. However, you can, of course, reveal your current thinking using the present tense. The point is to be sure to do justice to the work done and reported in the thesis first, and only to judge or amend your thinking, in the light of present understanding, after you have done so. Since the thesis is, at the time of the examination, very familiar to you, and its weaknesses are only too obvious, this line of thinking and speaking may take some practice.

Saying 'I'

In most published academic writing, including the thesis, it is not normal to use the first person singular, 'I'. Traditionally, and arguably, the intention was to create an impression of complete objectivity both in the presentation of results of research and in the research process itself. Although this practice is now debated, and although some top journals, such as the *British Medical Journal*, now require a more direct style, making clear who did what, for example, it is still the case that thesis writers in some disciplines are reluctant to use 'I'.

This is fine. Clearly, you have to use the conventions that operate locally, i.e. in your discipline and in your department. However, think about what the effect might be of you never, or rarely, saying 'I' during your examination. Will it be clear that you did the work yourself? If you use 'we', instead of 'I', will it be clear that you can be an independent researcher (one of the criteria of the doctoral examination)? Therefore, one of the activities you should practise in advance of your examination is talking about your work using the first person.

The active voice

The passive voice is widely used in academic writing, the active voice less so, although this is beginning to change in some areas. In the meantime, however, many academic writers stick with the formal passive: 'The work was completed' (passive), instead of 'I completed the work' (active).

For the examination, you might choose to continue with this style, as long as it is clear what you mean:

- The data were gathered . . .
- The analysis was conducted using . . .
- Chapter X was written with the intention of . . .
- It was suggested that . . .

Is it clear that *you* did these verbs? Are you failing to take credit for your own work if you use the passive throughout? Will you become, in a sense, invisible in your own study if you never use the active voice? Is the final example sufficiently clear: who 'suggested'? Your supervisor? Yourself? Another researcher? In your department? In the literature?

While these will seem, to some, theoretical questions, it is important to decide whether you are going to use the style of written academic English or whether it is appropriate to adapt your style for the spoken form. In some instances the passive voice is ambiguous. In others it is adequate for the purpose. Your decision may, of course, be influenced by the conventions of discussions in your discipline. However, it is probably safe to say that you are free to use different forms – including the active voice – in the examination. While it may be appropriate to 'write yourself out' of your thesis, it may be wise to 'write yourself in' to your discussion. Since it involves a change of style, this might take practice.

Stating the obvious

The section in this chapter called 'Correcting mistakes' (pp. 121–4) tells the story of a student who *appeared* not to know something that was obvious in her field of study. While that case is analysed in some detail, it is important to consider separately what 'stating the obvious' might mean and what it might involve for the student in the doctoral examination.

What is 'the obvious'? It is something that is understood – or taken – to be true by more or less everyone in the field. Or it could be something that is so well established that it is no longer open to question, no longer contested. Or it might be something that can be expected to remain true for some time in the field of study, among researchers or practitioners. It might have become 'true' from first principles in the field, or have come to be taken as a first principle.

This might be a legitimate – and important – line of questioning for the examination because it tests the student's knowledge of what is and is not contested in the discipline. The question of what is 'obvious' might also test the student's understanding of how – historically, chronologically, theoretically – something became 'obvious'. It also tests the student's ability to discuss, and by implication teach, basic principles. An examiner may go one step further, probing the student's understanding of the reasons for something being considered obvious. Or he or she might choose to challenge the candidate's acceptance of first principles, pressing for stronger, or more detailed, arguments.

Alternatively, it is possible that what is obvious to the thesis writer might not be obvious to the examiner. Because some parts of the thesis may have been written well before the examination, the student may lose perspective in some of the debates. Or the student may feel that some of the arguments have been so thoroughly thrashed out in the thesis that the point has already been made and requires no further discussion.

For example, the examiner might ask a question like 'Is this result more important than that one?', where the results have clearly occurred in a progression. It is, in a sense, obvious that one result led to another. It is obvious that the second would not have occurred without the first. But the candidate's task is to spell out that there was a progression, even to describe its features, the element of cause and effect and, finally, to answer the question: yes or no. Even though the key point, for the candidate, is that there is a progression, is one step in the progression more important than another? This is another example of having to rethink, even redraw, your written material in a new way.

However, although there are understandable reasons for perceiving certain issues and questions as obvious, it would be a mistake to treat the examiner's question *as if* it were obvious.

What not to do

- Treat the question as ridiculous.
- Appear amused by such a simplistic question.
- Express annoyance at such a basic question.
- Ask the examiner why they are asking you this.

Candidates, even though they know that every question requires a strong answer, may experience any of these reactions; the point is not to reveal them. Yet trying to suppress your feelings, and to hide them, is difficult, especially under pressure. Are you sure that you can do it well? Or can you, instead, adjust your perspective to the point that you accept that 'obvious' questions are important in research and scholarly writing and are, therefore, relevant in your discussion?

In some instances, as perhaps in the examples treated in the Jane Austen case below, the examiner may simply be trying to test you, to see if you can deal with a misinterpretation of what you have said or written. The examiner may act as if they have not read your work properly, as if they have taken the worst interpretation from it, but, rather than sitting seething or inwardly quaking, you still have to construct a strong answer, perhaps even more than one answer. That is your role.

Presentations

There is some disagreement among students about giving a presentation in a doctoral examination. There are pros and cons:

Pros	Cons
It lets you have your say	Anxiety
It puts you in charge	Examiner may interrupt anyway
You show closure and coherence	Technology may not work
You demonstrate knowledge	Too formal
A warm up for question-and-answer	Raises stakes
Point to highlights	Reveals weaknesses in presenting

Whatever your view on this debate, it is important to know that giving a presentation is an option. Some supervisors ask their students if they would prefer to give an opening presentation of 15 to 20 minutes. This can serve the same function as the opening summary. If the supervisor does not suggest it, the student can always ask. The decision might depend on local regulations and customs.

Pausing

It is good practice to pause occasionally while speaking, not necessarily for very long, but certainly long enough to take a deep breath every so often. There are several different types of benefits:

- helps you to control your voice;
- stops you from running on and on and losing track;
- forces you to slow down;
- stops you from missing a step in your argument;
- gives you time to think;
- lets you observe non-verbal feedback.

You can pause at several different points and for different purposes. To some, this may seem a bit contrived, but where is the logic in leaving this to chance? Success in this examination is, after all, about achieving the highest level of performance, and we all know that great performances require plenty of practice. So, rather than just making a mental note – 'I must remember to pause' – it helps to think more specifically about when and why.

When to pause
- Before you answer a question – time to think.
- During your answers – marks logical shift to next part of answer.
- Towards the end of your answer – do they want you to continue or stop?

The key benefit of pausing is that it can help you to control your anxiety levels. If you practise pausing to breathe, stopping for a second or two between sentences, you will also seem more controlled and careful in your speech, compared to someone who rattles on. In your enthusiasm – and enthusiasm is important – you may start to speed up again, but you can practise reminding yourself to pause for breath. At the very least, this will stop you straining your voice and sounding strained. If you have practised thoroughly, you should not sound strained. You will still be under pressure, but you will manage it well.

Highlighting strengths

How likely is any examiner to say, 'Please tell us how good this thesis is . . . and could you point out the best bits for us?' Not very likely. The examiner may well praise your work and writing, but it is just as likely that the discussion will focus on areas that require further development or revision. This is not to say that examiners are oblivious to the genuine quality of doctoral candidates' work; they are not. However, they are likely to be preoccupied with asking testing questions for obvious reasons. The viva is, after all, a test.

It may be up to the candidate, therefore, to draw attention to the highlights of the thesis.

Strategies for talking about strengths

* Which parts of your thesis are you proud of? Say so.
* Which parts do you want to highlight? Call them 'highlights'.
* Practise working them into your answers.

If you do not do this, the risk is that the idea of strengths may not come up or be considered, or, at worst, aspects of your work may not even be seen as strengths.

More specifically, there are certain key words that you must use, at some point in your examination, in relation to your work. While you must be careful not to overstate the quality of your work, and not to appear to be contradicting the examiner – unless you mean to – in pointing out the positives in your work, you must find ways to speak positively about it, using terms that 'brand' its strengths appropriately:

* Value
* Impact
* Benefits
* Strengths
* Effectiveness

- Contribution – of what type and scale?
- One way of solving the problem
- Trade-offs – strengths outweigh weaknesses.

Perhaps it is fear of claiming or appearing to claim too much credit or value in their work that makes candidates hesitant about using such terms. The purpose of the examination is, after all, for the examiner to decide if the work has any such value at all. If the candidate starts to attach value to aspects of the work, then they might appear to forestall the examiner's judgement.

What not to do

- Use all the key words above, as if they all fit your research/thesis.
- Assume examiners will see the strengths of your work.
- Assert them.
- Claim too much.
- Assume the examiner knows your thesis as well as you do.

Some people think that if the research is good enough it will speak for itself. There will be no need to 'sell' the work, to highlight its strengths, and so on. This might well be true in some areas. However, it might equally be true that the examiner would like to find out if you know what constitutes a strength, can draw his or her attention to it skilfully and can make a convincing case for it as a strength. This should not be hard to do, in theory. All this work has been done in the thesis. It should all be in the abstract, but some examiners and supervisors report that students are notoriously bad at writing about this sub-ject. However, constructing a verbal argument and holding the examiner's attention while you make it is another skill altogether.

Talking about weaknesses

> What if they ask if there are any weaknesses in my study? . . . Should I try to hide any weaknesses? . . . Will I fail if I say, yes?
>
> (Anonymous student)

Do all examiners ask, explicitly, about weaknesses? They may do so, but they may ask you why you did something and hope to draw you out, to prompt you to raise the question of weaknesses. This is not a ploy to manipulate you, nor is it an opportunity to cover up any weaknesses there are; instead, it is a test. The examiner wants to know if you are aware of the weaknesses. Are you sufficiently knowledgeable to see them as such? Can you talk about them coherently? Are you aware of how to avoid them next time?

The subject of weaknesses seems to produce a fair amount of anxiety among students facing oral examinations. This may, again, be the result of lack of information about how 'pass/fail' decisions are made in the examination. It also suggests that the idea of talking about weaknesses is challenging to students. The concept of talking about weaknesses positively is new.

Students are usually acutely aware of the weaknesses of their work; this is not new. We all know that all projects and all theses are, in some way, uneven. Usually, however, someone else tells students about the weaknesses of their work; what is new in this oral examination is that the students themselves have to talk about the weaknesses. What their anxiety might actually reveal is the students' recognition that this conversation will be assessed.

Some weaknesses will be the result of limitations in the study that were there by design. You put them there. You deliberately, and sensibly, focused your study at an early stage in the project. You decided to take a certain course of action in your research. Yes, it could be improved, but you did what was feasible (and agreed). After careful consideration, you set out to achieve a limited set of objectives.

The examination may require you to re-rehearse these decisions – made some time ago – as a coherent action plan. Rather than just doing what you could afford to do in the time you had, your work was a sensible, rigorous sequence of decisions. I hope you will have recorded such decisions and will be able to review your records before your examination (this is where a research journal comes in extremely handy – a pointer for students reading this at an early stage in their doctorate). If not, you will need to exercise your memory – and your supervisor's? – in order to revisit and recover these early rationales. The most important early decisions are, of course, recorded in your thesis and you should find a way of rehearsing arguments you have written there in speech form.

In your thesis every 'weakness' has its own corrective. Limitations can be explained as sensible decisions, within constraints, or documented as part of the research process itself. In a written text you are able to justify the work you did, to point out trade-offs for any apparent weaknesses and to show cogently and thoroughly how limitations do not undermine the value of your work.

By contrast, in discussion you have to do the following:

1 Rehearse these written correctives in speech form, convincingly.
2 Invent correctives – or other forms of argument – for weaknesses that were not accounted for in your thesis.

Matters may be complicated by the fact that, knowing what you know now, there are distinct weaknesses in your study. Perhaps you did not see them early on. Perhaps you did not agree that they were important enough to do anything corrective with them. Or perhaps you have only recently realized that there are weaknesses.

As a result, prior to your examination, you may be forming the impression that your thesis is seriously flawed. You may feel inclined to hide the weakness, or avoid talking about it, as much as possible. That, however, could be an error. If you appear to gloss over a weakness, once the examiner has asked you about it, you might appear not to have seen it, or, worse, not to realize how serious it is.

So what can you do? You can, of course, discuss weaknesses as weaknesses in order to do the following:

1 Demonstrate your understanding of what makes a good study.
2 Use contrast to emphasize the strengths of your study.
3 Show you understand the compromises involved in doing research.
4 Convince the examiners that you will address these weaknesses in future publications.

In an ideal world every study would have no weaknesses, but in the real world, it could be argued, that never happens. In effect, you have to find a way to normalize what you think are weaknesses, as far as possible.

Unexpected new weaknesses may, of course, be brought to your attention for the first time by the external examiner during your examination. It is not possible to anticipate everything they will choose to ask, or to pinpoint their perceptions of where the strengths and weaknesses of your work lie. This means that you should be ready for surprises – a contradiction in terms. Yet dealing with surprise questions could be considered a skill and is certainly something you can practise with peers: ask them to devise one or two questions. These may be follow-up questions. Once they have absorbed a few of your answers they may be prompted to ask a related probing question. Ask them to use the words 'weakness', 'deficiency' or perhaps even 'error' or 'serious omission' – without warning – in order to see how you react, cope and answer.

However, discussing weaknesses *as weaknesses* may be a new event for you. Previously, 'weaknesses' meant areas that you then went on to develop, strengthen or cut from your project or your writing. In other words, you still had time to do something about them. By the time you get to your examination, however, you cannot do anything about existing weaknesses. They are there for all to see. The examiner may simply want you to admit that you see them too.

Strategies for talking about weaknesses

1 Talk about them in terms of what you might do to strengthen an area of your study. Make a strong case orally for your research.
2 Discuss them in terms of what you would do to avoid them next time.
3 Represent them as inevitable in all research, stating exactly how they came to be, in your piece of work specifically.

4 Relate the weakness to your aims, showing how your original intentions were sound, based on good thinking and practice.
5 Admit that you knew you were taking a risk, but that there was a sound reason for persevering.
6 Show that despite the weakness you did achieve what you set out to do, or that the weakness itself threw up something interesting or important, perhaps not developed in your thesis.
7 Consider if and/or how the weakness provides directions for future research.

What not to do

- Give a general, resigned declaration that 'this happens in every study'.
- Blame your supervisor for the weakness.
- Blame your data.
- Say, 'that was beyond the scope of my study', without giving a cogent argument to support this statement.
- Dismiss what is identified as a weakness as unimportant.

Talking about weaknesses will only remain a new event if you do not consider what might be considered a weakness by a critical reader and how exactly you might deal with the subject. Which of these strategies makes sense to you – and your supervisor – what exact words will you use and what level of detail will you use in this part of the examination discussion, assuming that it comes up at all?

A useful strategy is to state that you might have been misleading in how you have written something, showing that what appears to be a conceptual confusion, for example, is actually a use of overstatement, perhaps claiming too much for a particular aspect of your research. You can, in other words, revise – and prepare to revise – parts of the thesis you are no longer happy with: for example, you could say, 'By saying X I meant . . .'. However, it is still important to show that what you have done has sufficient power to answer the research questions you set out with at the start of your doctorate.

You may also reveal in your answers more detail about the data, perhaps mentioning data that you did not include in your thesis. This is not fraudulent; researchers decide which data to use and how to analyse them. Sometimes a certain amount of 'smoothing' goes on in the interests of focusing on the main questions in the study. Data that have not been used for the thesis can be used for future investigations or future writing, after all. Some examiners will be aware of this and will want to explore this with you. It might be as well to be clear and honest in your answers, particularly if you have omitted contradictory data, for example. The outcome of such a discussion may well be that you have to reinstate the data in your thesis. Once again, however, your key answering strategy should be to continue to make the case for the work you have included in your thesis.

Finally, check – in discussion with your supervisor – that you are not exaggerating the weaknesses. Because your thesis is now quite 'old' for you, because you have, to some extent, moved beyond it and because you have been working on it for so long, parts, if not all, of it may seem weak to you alone. You will know your thesis better than anyone else and are likely to see its weak points much more clearly than any other reader. Relax. At least one other authorized person has deemed your thesis worthy of submission. It might not be as 'weak' as you think.

Whether the weaknesses of your study or thesis are major or minor, the point of this section is that you should be prepared to have a discussion of the weaker aspects of your work and writing. If you do not prepare for this type of interaction, you might answer the questions poorly. That would not look good. If, on the other hand, you have thoroughly prepared and rehearsed a few answers along these lines, then you are more likely to deal with questions, even if the examiner asks you about areas that you had not seen as weaknesses. Having read this section – and had some of these discussions – you may already find that the word 'weakness' has, to some extent, been normalized.

Hindsight

Looking back on your completed project, you must have much more knowledge than you did at the start. Surely it is safe to assume that all doctoral students will have learned something in the course of their studies that will make them realize they could have done things differently in their study. Surely there will be lessons learned along the way. This is called hindsight.

For some, this is frustrating: you have no sooner finished a phase of work than you realize how much better it could have been. However, others acknowledge that this is a fact of life. Hindsight is an important marker of your learning. It is therefore important that you demonstrate it in your examination, and this might mean using the word hindsight explicitly.

For example, it is legitimate to say in your examination something beginning with the phrase 'In hindsight I can see that . . .', to propose improvements – 'I would now . . .' – or to speculate about what might be a useful next step: 'I would speculate that . . . would lead to an improved outcome . . .'. Do not feel that you should represent authoritative knowledge only; you can also use more reflexive words, such as 'I have learned that . . .'.

In the doctoral process some would argue that there are certain lessons that can *only* be learned by looking back. Only by reviewing your work carefully, this argument goes, can you fully realize what you have learned. Take a good look back and think about what you might say about 'hindsight' in your examination. In other words, there may be some hindsight lessons that you still have to learn that are not in your thesis and that you should be ready to talk about in your examination. The hindsight perspective may also transform some aspects of your thesis, as you see things differently. This may mean that you will want to talk about them in terms different from those you have used in your writing. Clearly, this will require some preparation.

Citing

It can strengthen your answers if you can cite the work of authorities in discussions of your own work. This demonstrates that your research area is important.

However, you can go one step further with this standard strategy and make explicit connections between your work and that of others. If you can mention your work in the same sentence as theirs, for example, you have created an opportunity not only to bask in reflected glory, but also to make conceptual or intellectual connections between your work and that of more established researchers.

Some people see citing – and particularly self-citing – as just another aspect of one big academic game, but in the context of examination preparation it might make you establish your – admittedly limited – authority.

Correcting mistakes

The following narrative and commentary draw on the experiences of working with many students. Although the circumstances were narrated by one student, the case represents a type of misunderstanding that can develop in an oral examination. The case concerns a doctoral student in English literature, but there are lessons that can be taken from it for other subjects.

The purpose of this case is to send two simple, but crucial, messages to students preparing for doctoral examinations:

1 Your examination may not be a straightforward question-and-answer dialogue.
2 If you make a mistake during your examination, correct it.

Case study

They asked me a question on Jane Austen and . . . I can't remember how I answered it, but I thought it was OK. Suddenly, inexplicably, the examiner said, 'Well, if you can't see the irony in Jane Austen, then you've missed the whole point.'

I had no idea where she had got that from – of course I saw the irony. Everyone sees the irony. But I was too shocked and, to be honest, mystified, to correct her. Instead, we went on to the next question, leaving everyone at my oral assuming that I did not understand one of the most basic aspects of that subject.

I still do not believe that I said what she said I did, but I should have corrected her immediately. I now feel that I was positioned into 'giving a wrong answer'. I want everyone to know this story, so that they don't let it happen to them. If an examiner does this kind of thing, then the student has to rectify it . . . I passed my second oral, but I'll never forget the first one.

The first message we can take from this is that if something you say is interpreted wrongly, or if you cannot even work out how the examiner has taken such a point from what you have just said, you must do something about it immediately. You may not get a second chance. You may have to interrupt the next question and take the discussion back to the point where the problem arose. There are all sorts of reasons why this type of thing might happen: a lapse in concentration, testing you by saying something that is wrong, maliciousness, fatigue, jet lag.

On the other hand, if you have made a mistake, then you can correct it. Show that you understand that it was wrong. Rather than deciding that the situation is not recoverable, develop a new answer and point out that you are correcting an earlier wrong one.

Some students may think – or have heard – that it is better not to draw attention to their mistakes in this way. Let it lie, they argue, and perhaps no one will notice. Perhaps they will forget about it. This is a risky strategy, the risk being that your mistake is simply logged and weighed in the balance with your better answers, as in any other type of examination.

What does this story say about this student, about how she was positioned in this examination or about how she let herself be positioned? Does it say anything about the whole doctoral process experienced by this person? Or about this person's background, social or educational? How did she come to be unable, for that moment, to rectify the situation, to defend herself?

Perhaps she was used to being positioned in this way, had become conditioned to it, and had – perhaps temporarily – lost the ability both to recognize this and to access skills and strategies for working her way out of this position. Perhaps she had – consciously or unconsciously – begun to think 'I can't win'. She was, in effect, submitting to the examiner's superior power. Perhaps she simply did not have the skills for dealing with this kind of discussion. She certainly seems to have been unable to recover the situation once it had started to go wrong. This too might have been, for her, a familiar experience – she had been unable to assert herself in other situations. In other contexts, the consequence is that those who have power are simply confirmed in their roles, and sometimes that is fine. However, in the oral examination the consequences are very different for the student. Confirming your position of powerlessness, while understandable, is not a sensible strategy.

It is important to have strategies for when things start to go wrong – if they do, and for some they will not. For example, you have to show that you understand the examiner's concerns and convince him or her that you could do the necessary revisions and corrections to set things right. You may not be able to correct the weakness during your examination, but you can show them that you know how to go about correcting it after your examination. This requires you to think, in advance, of what you might do to strengthen your thesis. (You may already have discussed this with your supervisor.) The external examiner may want to pass you but still need to be convinced that you know what you have to do and, more importantly, that you have the ability to do it. If they feel that you cannot go any further with your work – or if they form the impression that you are not prepared to – they may feel that they have to fail you, even if they set out to pass you.

What does the case study tell us, if anything, about this examiner? Or about the other examiners present? Why did no one step in with a follow-up question to get the student back on track? Had they already decided to fail the student? We will never know what they were thinking. What we can do is prepare for questions – and responses to our answers – that misrepresent our knowledge.

Some may find the student's response to the situation a bit pathetic. She caved in under pressure. She did not fight back. To simply cave in like this – and not to understand why – is to deserve to fail. She simply did not perform well. In a sense, this may be true: the student did demonstrate an inability to construct a viable argument. If she had had more knowledge, then she could have shown that. She would not have buckled under scrutiny. She might have lacked confidence from the start because she knew that her knowledge was limited. Perhaps, deep down, she knew that she would not have much to say. Perhaps she found that she had nothing on which to base her counter-arguments, other than her sense of unfairness. Thankfully, she does not appear to have been so foolish as to believe that that answer would work in the oral examination. She certainly learned that her oral skills were poor, and this is why the case is included here. Even very bright people who write very well can be thrown by the new rigour of the oral examination.

This case characterizes the experiences of many students who have spoken about their fears before their examinations, and their experiences after the examinations. These students had not thought through what was going to happen in their examinations and had not prepared for the more probing questions. This narrative is intended as a wake-up call for those students who assume that oral skills developed in other contexts will see them through the doctoral examination. Unless they themselves have tested that assumption, they could be in for a rude awakening.

Finally, a quote from Tannen (1995: 291) offers a different perspective on what might have been going on in this case:

The difficulty of getting heard can be experienced by any individuals who are not as tenacious as others about standing their ground, do not speak as forcefully at meetings, or do not begin with a high level of credibility, as a result of rank, regional or ethnic style differences, or just personality, regardless of whether they are female or male. Whoever is more committed to compromise and achieving consensus, and less comfortable with contention, is more likely to give way.

It is likely that the candidate will perceive himself or herself as having less status than the examiners. Most students will, with some exceptions, approach the examination with a sense that they do not have a 'high level of credibility'. Many will feel uncomfortable with the idea of 'conflict' with the external examiner, even though they know that debate will almost certainly feature in their examinations.

This might explain the acute apprehension that many candidates feel in advance of their examinations: there is not only the conflict between how they like to behave and how they will have to behave, but also the conflict between themselves and their examiners.

Tannen's comments bring a new perspective to the case of the candidate described in this section: this candidate was not sufficiently 'tenacious', did not 'stand [her] ground', did not, understandably, feel that she began the oral examination with 'a high level of credibility' and was not comfortable disagreeing with the examiner. All these characteristics, particularly taken together, do not add up to a strong approach to this form of examination, a problem compounded, of course, by the student's lack of awareness of these issues.

The implication for other students facing their examinations is that they should define, illustrate and practise certain verbal, and non-verbal, behaviours well in advance of their examinations:

1 Exercising tenacity.
2 Demonstrating credibility.
3 Becoming comfortable with disagreement.
4 Balancing consensus and contention.

Of course, there may be other behaviours that students think are more appropriate for their examinations, but the main point is that all of these are designed to prevent the student caving in, in arguments, on the day of the examination. Given that the student may have become conditioned to accepting the supervisor's arguments, for example, this may require an adjustment: instead of automatically acceding to the examiner's every point and probe, the student has to be able to deflect some and dismiss others, through systematic debate, based on the work they have done.

Correcting yourself

If the examiner – as in the previous section – has formed an impression of one of your answers that you think reflects badly on you, or is plain wrong, then you must surely find a way to correct that, even at the risk of contradicting the examiner. You can do this by appearing to correct *yourself*, rather than appearing to contradict the examiner. You may feel that the last thing you want to do is confront the examiner – and you may be wise to think that – yet you have to ensure that any errors are corrected. Otherwise, they will influence at least the examiner's developing impression of you and your research and, at worst, the outcome of your examination.

Similar misunderstandings may have occurred with your supervisor or others to whom you were explaining your work. In fact, you may be thinking that you have tried all this with your supervisor and got nowhere, that you always have to give in, that they always have to be right. Again, it is important to see the doctoral examination as a distinctive event, very different from your interactions with your supervisor. This is not a developmental discussion; it is an examination.

Similarly, if you have contradicted yourself, you can correct yourself. Point out what you said that was contradictory: clarify and rectify.

Again, if the examiner wants to move on to the next question, you may have to defer your answer to that. Make it explicit that you are still answering the question, albeit an earlier one.

All of these strategies require that you play an active role. Instead of passively submitting to the examiner's interpretation of your answers, you ensure that your answers are not only well articulated but accurately represented. There is little point in providing, and performing, well-constructed answers if the examiner has not actually heard what you said, or has misunderstood it. Make sure that you listen carefully to the ways in which the examiner summarizes your answers, for example, or how they make the transition from your answer to the next question. If you feel you are being misrepresented, or 'positioned' wrongly or unfairly, then you should do something about it right away. In order to be ready to do this sort of correcting, you should practise this with a friend or colleague. You might want to start with a discussion of the 'Jane Austen' student. You might find that you have to rewrite the 'Jane Austen' problem to fit your context. What would you do? What exactly should you say if that happened to you?

Taking notes

Because students ask often enough and in large enough numbers whether they are 'allowed' to make notes during the examination, it seems important to point out that you can. There is no need to go into your examination without materials for taking notes, particularly if you like to scribble, list or mindmap as you think and talk about your work.

Taking notes during the examination can create any one of a number of impressions:

- you are listening carefully, attentive to the detail of the examiner's questions;
- you are an organized thinker, making a plan for your answer;
- you are a fluent writer, comfortable noting down ideas as they occur to you in the course of the discussion.

Examiners who like to be in charge may be content to see you positioning yourself as note-taker, as if you were attending one of their lectures. It is impossible to know exactly what they are thinking, and managing their perception of you might not be your priority.

On the day, during the examination, it can feel more comfortable to be looking down at your notes. It might help you to concentrate if you are not looking at the examiner all the time. You will be less likely to be distracted by non-verbal behaviours. You can avoid the tendency to stare at the examiner, which might give him or her the impression that you are challenging them. Some people will not want to maintain any eye contact with the examiner in any case, and taking notes is an alternative way of signalling that you are responsive.

Think about the layout of your notes in advance: you could have one side of the page for the examiner's question and leave the other side free for your answers. There could also be a third column to prompt you to be specific in your answers.

Notes layout		
Write down the question	**Notes for your answer**	**Specifics**
1 Summarize thesis . . .	Chapter 1 [verb] . . .	Elaborate . . .
	Chapter 2 [verb] . . .	Example . . .
2 Key people in the field?	Name (x ?) . . .	Date . . .
		Key idea . . .
		Key work . . .
3 . . . weaknesses in my thesis	Define . . .	Pros . . .
	Defend . . .	Cons . . .
		Alternatives

| 4 . . . how the work of . . . relates to my point on page . . . | Summary of point | Link . . . Difference . . . |

Taking notes in this format means that you will not fail to answer the question. While you may drift quite far away from it in your answer, if it is written in your notes in black and white you can always come back to it: 'So, to answer your question, the top three people in the field at the moment are . . .'.

How many times do you want to say, 'What was your question again?' Once? Certainly, you will not want to ask it more than once. You may be putting yourself under unnecessary pressure by trying to remember the terms of the question while simultaneously constructing an excellent answer. Being very knowledgeable, you may go into great depth in the course of your answer, yet fail to answer the question. The examiner may ask you the question again. Or there might be a new question. How will the examiner judge your failure to answer, or even remember, the question?

While you might not have time to write down the question word-for-word, you can always write down the essentials. This is not only good examination practice, it also saves you the labour, and perhaps stress, of trying to recall the exact terms of the question. You will be able to answer it explicitly, using the examiner's exact words. As in other forms of examination, using the words of the question is a good strategy for making sure you answer it.

Using notes during your examination might help you to elaborate in your answers, rather than just giving short answers only. You can also note down anything you feel you have forgotten to say in your answer, in order to remind yourself to insert an important point.

Just as in Chapter 3, where you were encouraged to write questions in different forms, you should also practise packaging, and repackaging, your answers in different ways. You could try using different structures for the same answer – for example, process, compare and contrast, problem and solution, question and answer, pros and cons for the same piece of information.

If you are skilled at answering questions without notes, then you will not need to take notes during your examination. In fact, you may want to give the impression that you do not have to take notes, that you have progressed beyond the 'write down the question' stage. You may, however, simply be sketching out several lines of response.

Whatever the form of the question, it is an invitation to talk about your thesis first and anything else second. The 'specifics' column should therefore remain the same – the work you have done, as described in the thesis you have written. The structure of your answer may change, along with the emphasis you give to certain aspects of your work. But the content remains fixed. The viva is, after all, an examination of the thesis. It is, of course, also an examination of your ability to talk about your work, perhaps in new ways.

Answering the question

One student in a recent viva workshop asked me if it was all right to ask the examiner a question. Such as?, I asked. Such as what he or she means by a term used in a question. My instinct was to advise the student not to do this. Why not? Examiners expect candidates to answer questions. If terms they use have more than one meaning, then that is part of the work of the examination: to deal with the potential multiplicity of terms, the complexity of research and the rigour of such discussions.

The specific question that the student was considering asking was, 'What do you think I should have done?' This would have given up the initiative to the examiner. It potentially takes the focus away from the work that has been done and puts too much emphasis on what might have been.

Instead of placing herself in the examiner's shoes, as part of her preparation, this student has asked the examiner to step into her shoes. The risk is that a completely different frame of reference will emerge, displacing the thesis that is being examined. Such a discussion will take time away from the student's excellent performance of her answers.

It is probably a good idea not to have too many questions for the examiner, and not to ask questions until you are asked to do so. There is a story about an examiner who walked out of a doctoral examination because he or she objected to the student asking questions: 'I'm here to examine you. This is not good practice.' Prepare specific questions to ask at this stage in your examination. This is not to say that you cannot ask any questions. If you are in any doubt, you can always ask if the examiner thinks it is appropriate for you to ask a question.

At the end of the day, the viva is another examination. Everyone who gets this far is good at passing examinations. Like any other examination, your task is to answer the question. Having covered some of the successful strategies for answers, the next step is to practise using them with realistic, thesis-specific questions.

Checklist

- There is a wide range of strategies for answering questions – pick ones that suit you and your work. Gather other examples from colleagues in your area.
- Think about how you could use more than one strategy to answer a question.
- Remember that the doctoral examination is not just simple question-and-answer; there will be more complex interactions – the subject of the next chapter.

7

Interacting

Debating • Non-verbals • Dealing with lack of feedback • Dealing with hostility • When examiners behave badly • Assertiveness • Being heard • Checklist

Debating

While you are writing your thesis you have to imagine the scholarly debate that you are joining by writing. When your thesis is read by someone else, it immediately enters that debate for real. In the doctoral examination, as in other presentations of your work to experts in your field, you experience the debate face-to-face.

Candidates and examiners spend much of the discussion debating different answers to the questions. For some students this is a new skill too; for others it will be the extended nature of the debate that is new.

As you prepare to engage in debate, you can identify the characteristics of academic debate in your area. What is it that is currently contentious in your area?

- Defining terms?
- Amassing different types of evidence?
- Contradictory evidence?
- The relationship of recent to previous studies?

Which of the current 'hot topics' are relevant to your work? Where do you stand in current debates? More importantly, how will you construct your position in the debate without appearing to demolish the opposition? You can prepare for this aspect of the examination by constructing cogent arguments against them.

Many of these features are already in your thesis. You can extract them for use in practice with peers and colleagues. Practise debating. This might require you to prepare a string of questions for them to ask you in succession. Practise staying with one issue over 10 minutes or so. Practise giving an account of the *relative* weight of different answers, approaches or analyses.

Non-verbals

Non-verbal communication and body language are, of course, culture-specific; shaking your head means one thing in one culture and the opposite in another. Even when it is possible to 'read' body language, we cannot be entirely sure what the person is thinking.

In the context of the doctoral examination, you can have an indication of the examiners' attentiveness, through the nodding of heads, the quality of the eye contact and, perhaps, the raising of eyebrows when they are interested. However, raised eyebrows can also signify surprise, even scepticism. If the examiners start to take notes, is that because they are interested in what you are saying or are they writing down a more probing follow-up question? If they look at each other, as you are speaking, does that mean that they agree . . . but what are they agreeing about? That you have answered well, or that you have answered badly? How can you possibly know for sure?

The important thing about body language in the examination is not to be distracted by it. You still have to concentrate on giving strong answers to questions. You may receive no positive cues at all, but as long as the examiners are not interrupting you, continue to construct your strong answer.

It might be worth thinking about your own body language too. Which non-verbal signals do you want – and not want – to give to your examiner? Will you use direct eye contact, signifying, to some, directness and, to others, hostility? Have you checked the effect your eye contact has on anyone lately? Will you go to the lengths of practising in a mirror? This would, at least, give you a real – rather than imagined – sense of what you look like. You could vary eye contact, looking down to your notes to signify thinking, and then looking up, when you say something like, 'So, to answer the question . . .'.

But this whole area is very personal, very subjective. Some will see it as insignificant; others will see it as one of the more important ways we have of communicating our – qualified – confidence in our work. And, after all, if we have no confidence in our work, who else will? As one colleague put it to me recently: 'Don't give them any ammunition.'

What are you going to do with your hands? Some people are very self-conscious about using gestures in their explanations, but if that is part of your personal style, why worry? You may want to watch out for simple stuff, like not crossing your arms, which, apparently, makes us look defensive, and sitting in a more open position. Then there is the debate about hands in pockets. Perhaps more for presentations, but perhaps also in the doctoral examination, people often feel that they do not want to look too relaxed, too informal or even disrespectful. This is, after all, a formal examination.

The relative formality or informality of the examination will, to a certain extent, be determined by the arrangement of the room. Some examiners or panels choose to arrange themselves quite formally around a table, while others go for a more informal set-up, with easy chairs and a low table. The main point is not to be fooled by the latter: some of the toughest doctoral examination experiences occur in the most ostensibly relaxed and comfortable settings.

You might, of course, choose to introduce a note of formality or professionalism to the proceedings by requesting a table or something to lean on while you take notes. If you are not comfortable with the arrangements you should say so, especially, if, for example, the sun is shining in your eyes, there is a lot of background noise, you are too close to a heater or the room temperature is too high or low for you. Any of these can affect your experience of the next two hours quite powerfully.

Dealing with lack of feedback

> I rallied my thoughts and stumbled through the answer. The examiner sat looking past me at the opposite wall, acknowledging my presence only by grunting at intervals.
>
> (Gordon 1952: 171)

Normally, when we answer a question someone has asked us, we get feedback from them in verbal and non-verbal forms. They react to our answer both while we are speaking and after we have finished. In the examination, however, you may find that once you have answered the question you get no feedback as to whether or not you have given the 'right' or 'wrong' answer, or whether your answer was adequate or not.

This lack of feedback can be disconcerting. You might wonder if you have made some error, annoyed the examiner in something you said or accidentally said something wrong or ridiculous without realizing it. As a result, you may be distracted from answering the next question, you may appear more uncertain of what you are saying and, when you realize that there is no feedback on your next answer either, you may think that they have already made up their minds to give you a negative result. You have to do something to prevent this negative thought spiral from starting. What you have to keep telling yourself is that your suspicions about what the other person is thinking are likely to be the result of your own projections. Do not waste time and energy trying to second-guess the examiners' thinking from their reactions.

In order not to be put off by this type of moment, it is a good idea to practise. '[The examiner] looked at me as if he was surprised to see me there, and every answer I made was received with the same expression. I found this most disheartening' (Gordon 1952: 171). It is unlikely that your examiners will be as indifferent as this. If they do seem to be losing concentration as you speak, you have to work at not letting it put you off. Besides, it may be happening for all sorts of reasons: an examiner may be thinking ahead, forming the next question, or recalling what you said in your thesis, or getting ready to articulate his or her own views. If you do feel yourself reacting negatively to the examiner's behaviour, remember that you can still mask your reactions. In fact, this is part of what professional dialogue is about.

If examiners did give feedback, in the form of nods, non-verbal cues to continue or even saying thank you as the student completed an answer, then the student might be able to relax and think more about what he or she was saying than about what the examiner was thinking. It is important not to waste time and energy trying to work out what they think; you simply have to get on with giving excellent answers.

Dealing with hostility

A graduate student's examination is not the right place to practise the academic equivalent of the martial arts.

(Delamont et al. 1997: 145)

Chapter 6 provided strategies for dealing with different types of 'difficult' questions and 'correcting' poor responses. What should you do, however, if you encounter direct hostility? As sensible as Delamont et al.'s advice is, there are, unfortunately, still occasions when questioning does turn hostile, or at least is perceived to be by the candidate. It is important to acknowledge that as the questions get harder, more probing, you may perceive them to be hostile.

You can defuse hostility by nodding, perhaps writing down a note, even saying, 'Yes, I can see what you're saying.' This works because when people are hostile it is often because they are trying to force a point home. The examiner may simply want you to acknowledge his or her point of view. You might want to make a concession, acknowledging that there is room for improvement. If this works, you can still reassert the value of the work.

If, however, the external or internal examiner combines negative comments on your work and/or your answers with repeated interruptions, a string of questions that are beyond the scope of your study and negative body language, such as shaking the head, sighing, frowning or laughing at you – all of which add up to what you feel is a hostile environment – what will you do? What would you prefer to do?

- Endure it, and appeal later?
- Ask them to stop being hostile?
- Appeal to the supervisor to intervene?
- Switch to a more assertive style yourself?

The last of these may be what the examiner is looking for. If you can think on your feet, you might be able to work out what is bugging them: is it something you said in one of your answers? They may simply be pressing you to accept that an alternative approach might work, even if you feel it is not directly relevant to your study.

Above all, remember that there is no need for you to become hostile or defensive yourself. Nor do you have to break down under their 'inquisition'. Stay calm, keep breathing and keep talking. This will take practice. If you do not practise this, you will be under much more pressure.

When examiners behave badly

Clearly, this should not happen at all, and with the increasing use of an independent chair in doctoral examinations, even if it did happen, it should not be the student's role to manage it. However, students have apprehensions. 'Worst case scenarios', however irrational, can affect students' performance, and are therefore worth thinking through. Review coping strategies. Coping involves two levels: managing your reactions and managing others.

Once an examiner starts to behave badly, the student has a number of options:

- Ignore it. Respond to the question, don't react. Stay calm.
- Ask the examiner to stop behaving that way – say that you find it difficult/ disturbing/distracting.
- Ask the chair/supervisors to intervene.
- Say that you feel the examiner's behaviour is affecting your performance, if you feel it is. For example, if the examiner constantly interrupts you, all your answers will be incomplete.

These are not the only options, of course – you may want to take advice on this subject from others. Your choice of response – or non-response – will depend on a number of judgements: how bad the problem is, how appropriate you feel it is for you to mention it, how comfortable you are with the more combative style of debate, how ready you are to negotiate with the examiner and/or the chair.

The main point is clearly not to let the examiner's behaviour affect your performance. This is easier said than done, given the power dynamic in the doctoral examination. In terms of preparation, the main point is to practise with a more aggressive style of questioner, so that you can work out for yourself what you would do. It may never happen, but working through your 'worst case scenarios' is a good way of defusing your apprehensions.

Assertiveness

> You are clearly in the hot seat – although this is your day, it is the time to perform. You need to be assertive about your knowledge, clearly in command of all that you did and of the professional literature which informs your understanding.
>
> (Brause 2000: 139)

Assertiveness and aggressiveness are often taken to mean the same thing. In fact, there is overlap in the definitions. Those who see assertiveness as 'getting what you want' will, of course, link it to aggression. However, being assertive means saying what you want and accepting other people's responses. We can use the quotation from Brause above to point out a useful distinction between being 'in command' either of the examination or the examiners, which is not your goal, and being 'in command' of your work and your thesis, which is.

In the context of the doctoral examination, this means asking an aggressive examiner to stop being aggressive; if you do not ask, they will not hear. They cannot read your mind. They may feel that they are just being enthusiastic, or rigorous, or both. The beauty of assertiveness is that it stops us from sending all sorts of covert, non-verbal signals. If you are unhappy with the examiners' behaviour, the thinking goes, then you will reveal that. So you might as well keep things clear and say what you think.

Research suggests that there are gender issues in the doctoral examination (Leonard 2001). There are, of course, other groups, who are under-represented in the profession and among external examiners, who face similar problems. It is not unknown for candidates in these groups to feel that they are being patronized. If you feel you are being talked down to, you may choose simply to accept and endure that; however, if you feel that your work is undervalued, then you may want to challenge that point. Even if your work is modest, there is no reason why you should be treated condescendingly. Given all the work you have done, it can be offensive when someone treats you as a complete novice. In most cases, this will not happen. But what would you do if it did?

- Rephrase your point.
- Do not be defensive or dogmatic.
- Make explicit links to the question you were asked.

Just because you are being treated as if you were some kind of second-class citizen of academe does not mean that you have to alter your behaviour. Nor can you expect to change the behaviour of the examiner who is patronizing you. Not in the space of two hours anyway.

Being heard

Deborah Tannen (1995), in a chapter on direct and indirect speech patterns, uses an example of the lead-up to a plane crash to illustrate how we can go about *not* making ourselves heard:

> Among the black-box conversations . . . was the one between the pilot and co-pilot just before the . . . crash. The pilot . . . had little experience of flying in icy weather. The co-pilot had a bit more, and it became heartbreakingly clear on analysis that he had tried to warn the pilot, but he did so indirectly . . . The co-pilot repeatedly called attention to the bad weather and to ice building up on other planes . . . He expressed concern early on about the long waiting time between de-icing . . . Shortly after they were given clearance to take off, he again expressed concern . . . The takeoff proceeded, and thirty-seven seconds later the pilot and co-pilot exchanged their last words.
> (Tannen 1995: 92–3)

While there are obvious differences between flying a plane and taking a doctoral examination, there are similarities in the potential tension over direct and indirect speech. Moreover, one of the reasons for being indirect – difference in status – is common to both. This relates to points about assertive speech in the previous section. The point is that it is important to consider whether speech patterns that you may have been using for some time in discussions with your supervisors, peers and colleagues in your area are appropriate for your examination, or not.

Differences in status include gender differences, also discussed in the previous section. Without going into full sociolinguistic analysis, we can agree that some speech patterns are more likely to be heard and that others are less likely to be listened to:

> Although the ways women speak may contribute to their not being listened to, research shows that, all else being equal, women are not as likely to be listened to as men, regardless of how they speak or what they say.
> (Tannen 1995: 284)

Naturally, everyone involved in higher education denies that there is anything like deliberate discrimination of the type that this quotation from Tannen will seem to some to imply. However, it is clear, from the employment statistics of any organization, for example, that there are discriminatory forces at work. Whether or not we are aware of the ways in which we treat each other differently because of a series of personal features, including gender, we must face up to the fact that we may contribute to our not being listened to. By 'we' I mean men and women who choose to adopt – or by default adopt – certain speech patterns.

Although Tannen suggests that we may be able to make little if any impact on stereotypes by changing our speech patterns, it is worth trying. There are many ways of speaking directly, including those that Tannen defines as different ways of saying the same thing, often with quite opposite effects. She suggests several options:

> Succinct so as not to take up more . . . time than necessary . . . with or without a disclaimer, loudly or softly, in a self-deprecating or declamatory way, briefly or at length, and tentatively or with apparent certainty . . . [We can] initiate ideas or support or argue against ideas raised by others. When dissenting, [we] may adopt a conciliatory tone, mitigating the disagreement, or an adversarial one, emphasizing it.
>
> (Tannen 1995: 279–80)

These are useful as a set of options for dealing with viva interactions: are you going to choose one set of options, or will you be able to choose options from both lists, according to what is appropriate at the time? The latter suggests that you will be able to think on your feet, choosing the appropriate speech pattern instinctively. It might be a good idea to prepare four or five types of response that you know you can draw on, depending on what is asked. You might, for example, choose to use more conciliatory speech patterns in the initial stages, rather than going straight to 'adversarial' forms. You might, in other words, foresee your responses as a sequence, with those at the start of the examination taking a different form from those towards the end.

Tannen (1995: 279) illustrates the patterns of disclaimers in practice:

- I don't know if this will work, but . . .
- You've probably already thought of this, but . . .
- This may be a silly naïve question, but . . .

Disclaimers help speakers to avoid seeming arrogant. The speaker is trying to avoid seeming to claim too much credit – if any – for his or her own ideas. While each of these responses might preface a strong and articulate response, they might also signal lack of confidence, on your part, in your answers.

Using disclaimers is one way of saying something, perhaps several times, and not being heard. What might be heard most clearly is your tentativeness. Often this happens to those who have less status than those who are listening-but-not-hearing. This can happen in many contexts and for many reasons.

Listeners may simply hear what they want to hear. Or, if they have already formed a judgement about you, they may not hear anything that appears to contradict that judgement. Or they may be preoccupied by something else. Or they might be reluctant to consider the implications of what you say.

In the examination it is your job to make the examiners listen. If you find that they seem to be ignoring you regularly, that is very serious. If it happens once or twice, less so. Has it happened to you before? Was that because of how you spoke? Is it about speaking with authority? Do you struggle to speak with authority, especially when you are speaking to an authority? Or, alternatively, does it say as much about them as it does about you?

If, during your examination, you find that you have said something that was not heard, should you repeat it? Should you restate it? If the examiner moves on to the next question, can you backtrack? Can you weave the answer that was not heard into the discussion of the next topic? These questions are not meant to spark a debate about what is and is not 'allowed' in the doctoral examination. These strategies are all legitimate. The question is, quite literally: can you do any of these things effectively? Which one suits your personal style best? Which one does your supervisor think is most appropriate? And, most importantly, how do you know that you can do any of these if you have not already practised them, not in other contexts, but for the new context of your examination?

Some students will, of course, have no problem saying precisely, and strongly, what they think. Some will have no qualms about engaging in argument with the examiner. They will not use the disclaimers discussed above, but will have developed a more assertive style, featuring, perhaps, such expressions as, 'It is obvious that . . . Note that' (Tannen 1995: 280).

While Chapters 5 and 6 dealt with questions and answers separately, this chapter has covered interactions that can occur in the oral examination, with the emphasis on the candidate adopting, quite deliberately, strong strategies for getting their points across. A critical theme throughout all three chapters has been the need to practise whichever strategies are selected as appropriate to a particular examination. The next chapter suggests what that practice should involve.

Checklist

- Do not try and guess what the examiner thinks about your answers from his or her non-verbal behaviours.
- Difficult questions may be asked, or may appear to be asked, in a difficult style or tone.
- Practise interacting – not just question-and-answer – with colleagues, peers, etc.

8

Practising

Re-reading your thesis • Practice session • A doctoral examination workshop • Mini-vivas • Mock viva • Talking to other students • Websites • Practising your 'set' of questions • Graduated practice • How to fail your oral examination • Checklist

> Few candidates seemed to do more [to prepare] than to re-read their thesis. Although one respondent wrote that her supervisor had told her that she could not prepare for her viva since 'everyone's viva is different', this was not sensible advice. Candidates need to know their thesis thoroughly, anticipate the kinds of questions that might be asked and have their answers ready should they arise.
>
> (Hartley and Jory 2000b: 21)

These points have been thoroughly argued in the preceding chapters. The need for realistic practice sessions has been argued in some detail. The central purpose of practice should be to 'unpack' the thesis, to disaggregate it into its components. This does not mean simply taking the chapters separately, though that too is important, but also disaggregating the logic and argument that you have worked so hard to create. You can use Chapters 5 and 6 to convert your thesis from a *single* coherent argument into a *series* of questions and answers. Once you have done this, you are ready for discussions with those who have pulled your work apart, the examiners.

Some students report that they had no practice at all before their examinations; for others a 'mock viva' is standard practice in their departments. This chapter recommends that systematic practice – with repeat practices – does take place, and provides guidance for students and supervisors on what this might involve. The concept of 'graduated practice', where the student builds up to a realistic rehearsal, is defined and illustrated.

The first step is to consider the shift from 'corrective' or developmental discussions about the thesis, which have featured in countless discussions between student and supervisor, to a discussion among experts who are testing the thesis. This is an important transition. The nature of the discussion can change quite dramatically. Up to this point the student might have become conditioned to taking on board each and every suggestion for alteration to the study and the thesis, as part of a process of ongoing critique. However, the oral examination is an opportunity to draw a line under this mode and defend the work as done. Many students will have been doing this for some months before submission, explicitly discussing 'closure' with their supervisors. The shift required for the oral examination is a continuation of this change process. For students, you still have to take on board feedback, but certain questions about what you have done will be used as prompts for defending it, rather than suggestions for changing it.

For example, you may have to reorientate 'What about trying . . .?' from a suggestion that you try something different in your research to an invitation (1) to define what you did; (2) to justify it; and (3) to consider the pros and cons of the alternative the examiner proposes. In other words, practise with even very familiar questions, so that you can deliberately manage this reorientation.

Show that you understand the quality of closure that you have already created. Show that you understand what the extra or alternative work would involve and what its outcomes might be, but, again, represent the work you have done as sufficient.

Re-reading your thesis

Although the case has been made that simply reading the thesis is not in itself enough, it is an essential first step in the process of re-engagement with the text. It does not just mean re-reading the thesis as if it were a book, from start to finish. Instead, it means reading it as a text that is soon to be examined.

For each chapter

- Read the chapter from start to finish.
- Write one sentence about it. This will act as a prompt for your thinking and recall.
- Put single-word prompts in the margin. This will help you to find your way if you lose your place.
- Convert the chapter into a series of questions and answers.
- Use these in your practice sessions.

In this way, you are not only revising all the elements of your thesis, and all the connections between them, but also, and perhaps more importantly, disaggregating your thesis, breaking it up and getting ready to consider the elements from different angles. This is not to say that you have to do any rewriting at this stage; leave that until you see what the examiner wants you to do in the way of revisions. Instead, you can prepare for different types of questions and different types of talk in your answers. In this way you will be less likely to be thrown or confused by the examiner's questions.

Towards the end of the examination, if the examiner says, 'I think you need to strengthen the section on . . .', you need to know your thesis well in order to be able to tell whether or not you have dealt with the proposed 'strengthening' in another chapter. You will know your thesis better than any examiner if you revise it well, and will be able to make a stronger case for it as it is.

On the other hand, if you do not know it well, and have forgotten exactly where certain subjects are dealt with in your own text, you will not appear very competent, you may have to do needless revisions or, in the worst case, you may be suspected of not having written the thesis yourself.

Practice session

In order to get the most out of a practice session, and in order to make the best use of your time and the time of those who are helping you to practise, make time for briefing and debriefing.

Briefing involves setting out, before the practice session, what you want to achieve, which activities you want to practise and the roles everyone involved in the practice session are expected to play. This may include going over sample questions, so that, for example, the person playing the examiner role knows how to pronounce certain words. For later sessions, they may need time to plan how to ask certain questions you have prepared in a different form. They might want to prepare their interruptions and probing follow-up questions.

Debriefing involves assessing the extent to which you did what you set out to do and evaluating the strengths and weaknesses of your performance. Equally important is the setting of new goals for future practice sessions. In fact, there are some things that will only become clear to you once you have started to practise. It is extremely unlikely that you will improve all your skills in one single practice session, although this is often the most that a supervisor will provide. Besides, you also have to take on board the feedback of your colleagues. However, you may find that they are not as hard on you as you are on yourself, and this can increase your confidence.

How can you practise for the oral examination?

- With friends. With anyone.
- With postgraduates in your area, or any area.
- With a postgraduate who has had their examination.
- With your supervisor(s): 'mock viva'.

One-hour practice session

- Aims: discuss what you want to achieve in your practice.
- Which skills do you want to develop or improve?
- Which strategies do you want to practise?
- Prepare questions: easy, hard, follow-up, probing.
- Run the examination as if for real, for one hour, without stopping.
- After this, have a full debrief: how did you do?
- How do they feel you did?
- Where do you need more practice?
- When can you practise this again?

A doctoral examination workshop

A workshop to help doctoral students prepare for their examinations could or should include three key elements:

1 An overview of research on the doctoral examination.
2 Definition of terms and local practices.
3 Practice session.

A programme for a three-hour workshop, including tutor presentations and student discussions, could be as follows.

Doctoral examination workshop programme: 3 hours

Session 1

9.30   Introduction, rationale, aims, scope
9.40   Definitions
        Expectations
        Approaches
        University code of practice
        Variations
        Examiner's report form

10.45   Break

Session 2: Practical

11.00   Answering questions:
      1 Participants write different types of sample questions, relevant to
        their theses.
      2 Participants practise using recommended answering strategies.
12.00   Discussion of the practice session: lessons learned, practice needed.

Session 3

12.15   Planning: countdown to the examination
      Further reading/viewing
      Checklist: practice
12.30   Conclusions and evaluation

Session 1, from 9.30 to 10.45, includes discussion of the university's code of practice, including, usually, questions about appeals procedures. *The Handbook for External Examiners* (UCoSDA 1993) is a useful reference point here, and students are usually keen to have their own copy of pages 76–7, the lists of questions examiners may ask about each chapter or phase of their thesis.

A video of a real examination, if any are available, or of the closest thing to it (Murray 1998), is helpful in getting students to visualize exactly the types of behaviour and environment they are likely to see in their examinations. It will help some to make the transition from informal discussion with their supervisors to the, usually, more formal discussion with their external examiner.

Session 2, from 11.00 to 12.00, involves students writing examples of questions and then practising answering them in twos. Students write one 'hard' and one 'easy' question and then ask a colleague to ask them each one in turn. The key here is that the questions should be specific to the thesis. Alternatively, students can practise with some of the other forms of question – and answer – listed in Chapters 5 and 6 of this book.

Session 3, 12.15 to 12.30, introduces the idea of the countdown to the examination, dealt with in Chapter 4, with an emphasis on encouraging students to plan further practice sessions.

Mini-vivas

In departments where the annual doctoral review includes an oral examination element, or mini-viva – a shortened form, but with similar assessment purposes and criteria – students and supervisors speak very positively about its value. More and more departments seem to be adopting this practice. While there is a perceived risk of frightening the student with such 'hard' assessment of their work in progress, in practice, these mini-vivas make students realize that 'You really have to understand everything you've written in your report'.

If, therefore, you are in your first or second year, and if your department does not operate this system, it would be beneficial for you to experience an examination in this form, no matter how little you feel you have to report, or how modest you feel your progress has been. The alternative is to wait until your final examination for the *first* oral examination of your work.

The content of a mini-viva may depend on the nature of your research and the discipline in which you work, but oral examination of your early writing on the literature, your evolving method or approach or your developing thoughts about how you will analyse your data sets can provide the motivation for you to revise and consolidate your learning about your field in ways that producing and discussing text might not.

The time that a mini-viva takes could also vary, but experience suggests that the first mini-viva, towards the end of the first year, might be quite long, two hours or more, with the second, towards the end of the second year, often being shorter, i.e. 30 minutes. However, practice varies. Check your department's regulations.

Carless (2002: 356) used mini-vivas in an undergraduate course for the purpose of emphasizing 'a continual process of learning', providing feedback to students that would emphasize 'improvement rather than solely the grading function'. These oral examinations lasted for 15–20 minutes, ran with groups of three students and allowed them to clarify and justify their approaches in their assignments. The questions asked were not unlike those that occur in doctoral examinations, ranging from the general 'Can you summarize . . .?' to the more probing 'What did you mean by statement X on page Y' and 'On page A you said B . . . Can you justify that statement?', to the detailed question about usage in 'Can you identify a grammatical problem in sentence two on page 3?' These questions were chosen to suit the lecturer's aims in teaching this course. Carless (2002) illustrates the educational value of mini-vivas and shows that they can take different forms, according to purpose.

Mock viva

If mock vivas are not arranged for them, then candidates should request them.

(Hartley and Jory 2000b: 21)

The definitive tone of this quotation is an indication of how important they are in preparing students for the real thing. In a similar vein, the Higher Education Funding Council of England endorsed a recommendation that all students should be offered a 'practice session' (Metcalfe et al. 2002: Annex D).

Delamont et al. (1997: 150–1) provide useful guidance on different types of mock viva, complete with handouts. They also suggest videotaping, to allow detailed discussion of the student's performance.

The mock viva should be an occasion when you bring together all the strategies outlined in these chapters. It should be close – in time and content – to the real thing:

- Arrange the room in the way that it is likely to be in your examination, possibly in the same room.
- Think consciously about your body language, your tone and other aspects of your performance as the mock viva proceeds.
- Monitor how you respond to questions and other interactions.
- Rehearse the full range of questions and answers.
- Remember to debrief afterwards.

A recent study showed that, as in so many aspects of the doctoral examination, there are 'considerable disparities in procedures within and across institutions' (Hartley and Fox 2004: 727). The more important finding may be that 90 per cent of students in this study found mock vivas helpful.

Talking to other students

For many students, those who have had their examinations are the only available source of information on what actually happens. But how reliable are their memories and how relevant are they to anyone else's examination? To what extent can we take their accounts at face value? Some will provide useful information; others will perpetuate the myths.

In addition, there is evidence that the outcome of the examination significantly influences students' accounts: those who pass with minor revisions are more likely to have positive memories of their examinations than those who pass with major revisions (Hartley and Jory 2000a).

What might be worth discussing is the extent to which department or national guidelines were followed. The forms that questions took might help to focus your mind in your preparations. There may be discipline-based patterns of which you were unaware, such as the timing of the announcement of the examiner's decision. Strategies that students used – or developed on the spot – and that seemed to work well would be useful to know.

All these topics would be important to take time to discuss, both with the student who is providing the report and with your supervisor.

Websites

There are many websites in which students report their experiences of the doctoral examination, some positive, some negative. Again, this is an important source of information about what actually happens, but it also has to be considered carefully.

Some websites are specifically intended to help students to prepare a thesis and prepare for the oral examination. For example, Joseph Levine has a helpful account of the processes (http://www.learnerassociates.net/dissthes/#30). He also lists useful sites at other universities and in other countries.

Kerlin (1998) explores the competitive element that is perhaps most obvious in the doctoral examination, but, it could be argued, pervades academic life (http://kerlins.net/bobbi/research/myresearch/health.html).

Practising your 'set' of questions

In Chapter 5 the idea of students, ideally with their supervisors, creating a personal 'set' of questions was introduced.

The purpose of developing a personal 'set' is to reduce and render more specific the long list of questions covered in Chapter 5. These questions can be customized to suit your research. Your practice should clearly focus on those types of questions that are directly relevant to your work.

Graduated practice

Although it is important to experience realistic practice, there is no need to rush into a 'mock viva' as your first step. What types of practice do you need? How much is feasible in the time you have? Do you have time for both 'experience preparation' and 'specific preparation' (Potter 2002)? Take time to consider the development stages you might want to work through:

1 Discussion with recent doctoral graduates, running some of your questions and answers past them.

2 Question-and-answer practice with supportive colleagues and friends, building your confidence.
3 Writing complex questions for more focused practice.
4 A mock viva with your supervisor.
5 Repeat practice sessions with any of the above asking the questions, developing a style that suits you.

This is, of course, a matter of personal choice. Some candidates might feel that they do not want to waste time in these earlier stages. Whatever your development stages, be sure to repeat the later practice sessions as often as you can stand to.

However, the term 'graduated practice' refers to a planned series of practice sessions of increasing difficulty. For example, a series of practice sessions could take up to 90 minutes, including short breaks and debriefing discussions, to move through four steps: easy and difficult questions, follow-up questions, aggressive questions and debate. These practice sessions can be done in doctoral student peer groups, with students taking turns to be examiner and candidate.

Step one involves writing two questions, one easy, one difficult, specific to your thesis. (You can use or adapt questions from Chapter 5.) Give your questions to your colleague to ask you. Answer the questions. This works well if you are both preparing for doctoral examinations – you can take turns to ask each other questions.

Step two is to take the difficult question and write follow-up questions, give these to someone to ask you. The person who is going to ask you the questions first changes some of the words – using different terms, adding a preamble, making the question longer and more complex, for example – then asks you the questions in these new terms. He or she also adds other questions.

Before moving on to step three, take five or ten minutes to debrief: tell your colleague how you felt doing this and how you feel you performed. What do they have to say about your performance? Did you answer their questions?

Step three is where you practise with a more negative examiner, one who interrupts, has what could be interpreted as negative or disinterested non-verbal behaviours, such as lack of eye contact or shaking the head. Your colleague can also practise being aggressive, interrupting you, saying things like 'You have not answered my question' or 'I think we're at cross-purposes here', or 'That's not very convincing.' These are legitimate responses in an academic discussion and appropriate responses in a formal examination, but in a certain tone, and in the context of the doctoral examination, they may appear aggressive. In your actual examination, the examiner may simply be speaking in strong terms because he or she is engaged by your work or your ideas. Or he or she may actually be aggressive. In this practice session, there may be smiles all round initially, as colleagues take on this aggressive role, and their reaction may be about unfamiliarity – a potential feature of all of these exercises – but it may also be a response to the added level of stress that this exercise brings for the person playing the student role. Consequently, your colleague may need a minute to think himself or herself into this role.

Again, as above, take a few minutes to debrief after this practice session.

Step four is practising debate, where you discuss pros and cons, give and take, review different answers to questions, while still answering the examiner's questions. Remind yourself what the terms of academic debate on your subject are likely to be: use of terms, use of evidence, strength of evidence, relative strength of other evidence, competing evidence, your experience in the field, the value of your evidence, scale of your research. This debate may involve taking you, the student, to the limits of your knowledge – how would you articulate that? Do you just say, 'I don't know anything, or any more, about that'? You may need a few minutes to prepare the terms of this debate and to coach your colleague on points and questions they will use. Some of these may draw on the discussions you had in steps one to three.

Again, debrief on this specific practice session and on all of them, taken together:

- What range of strategies do you think you have now practised?
- What have you not yet practised in these exercises?
- Is there anything you personally think you still need practice in?
- What is your colleague's assessment of your performance?

While this sequence of practice sessions works well to take students through a gradually increasing level of difficulty, it is important not to see these as one-offs. There is huge value in repeating these activities until you feel your skills have improved, and, perhaps, until feedback from your colleague confirms your judgement.

While many doctoral students think that this type of practice is only possible, or useful, with people who know their subjects well, it is important to note that these practice sessions work just as well, and sometimes better – in the sense of helping students to develop their skills – with a range of people, including other students in your discipline, students in other disciplines, friends, family, etc. The aim is to develop the ability to respond in an appropriate manner, whatever the question, whatever the examiner's tone and whatever you take from that tone. Experience of many doctoral examination preparation work-shops suggests that this aim is achieved in this type of graduated practice.

How to fail your oral examination

Here is a scene from C. P. Snow's novel *The Affair*:

At the first sight, entering the dark end of the room, Howard looked pale, ill-tempered, glowering . . .

'Good morning,' said Crawford, 'do sit down.'

Howard stood still, undecided where he should go, although there was only the one chair vacant in front of him . . .

Polite, active, Dawson-Hill jumped up and guided Howard into the chair . . .

Then he had gone off to Scotland to do research under Palairet? Why?

'I was interested in the subject.'

'Did you know him?'

'No.'

'You knew his name and reputation?'

'But of course I did.'

It would be fair to say that he had been impressed by Palairet's reputation and work? I had to force him. Just as young men are when they are looking for someone to do their research under? Was that fair? I had to press it. Reluctantly and sullenly, he said yes.

'When you arrived in his laboratory, who suggested your actual field of work?'

'I don't remember.'

'Can't you?'

Already I was feeling the sweat trickle on my temples. He was more remote and suspicious even than when I talked to him in private. 'Did you suggest it yourself?'

'I suppose not.'

'Well, then, did Palairet?'

'I suppose so.'

I persuaded him to agree that Palairet had, in fact, laid down his line of research in detail, and had supervised it day by day . . .

Some of the results he, or they, had obtained were still perfectly valid, weren't they? A longer pause than usual – no one's criticised them yet, he said.

(Snow 1960: 210–12)

There are, of course, a number of ways to fail your examination:

- Do not pick up on the examiner's cues to extend your answers.
- Go into your examination on the defensive.
- Convince yourself that the examiners are out to get you.
- Be paranoid.
- Give 'slow and strained, and . . . equivocal' answers (Snow 1960: 213).
- Throw questions back to the examiner.
- Show reluctance to engage in debate about your work.
- Get angry.
- Critique the system.

- Give one-word answers.
- Show disrespect for the examination itself.
- Get so tired that any of the above might happen.

Checklist

- Learning recurring questions and effective answering strategies is all very well, but only practice can improve your performance.
- Practise with a range of different people – anyone who will help. People in other disciplines and even non-academics can be more useful as 'mock examiners' than you might think.
- Don't just do one type of practice – do several, with increasing levels of difficulty. Repeat.

9

Outcomes

Waiting in the corridor • Decisions • Revisions and corrections • Appeals •
Recovery • Celebrations • Anti-climax • Endnote for students

Check your institution

This chapter runs through the types of outcomes of the doctoral examination, with the usual proviso that institutions use different terminology and,
potentially, procedures at this stage, as at all the previous stages.

A popular misconception is that the oral examination is the end of the doctoral process; this is often not the case. The stages that usually occur beyond
the examination are outlined, in order that you will be: (1) psychologically
prepared for what might feel like 'a fail'; and (2) mentally prepared to check
exactly what further work you have to do after the examination. You are
thereby likely to start revisions and/or corrections earlier and get through
them more quickly.

Waiting in the corridor

Not everyone is sent out of the room at the end of their examination, to wait in
the corridor, and if you are sent out do not take it as a bad sign. In some
institutions it is the norm, while in others you are told the result right away.

Find out which practice is used at your institution in advance so that you are prepared for it.

Sympathetic supervisors will be conscious that, for students, the moments between exiting the room and being called back in to hear the examiner's decision will not be easy. Since departments do not have a 'viva waiting room', students are likely to be standing in a corridor or an office nearby. Some students will prefer to spend the waiting time alone; others will want company. It would be as well to book your supportive company in advance, in case you end up spending this difficult spell with someone who makes you feel even more uncomfortable. Remember that although the formal examination has finished, you will still need to have your wits about you for the important discussion of revisions and corrections.

Decisions

There are a number of potential decisions that examiners can make at your examination, and there are a number of different terms for them in use at different institutions.

It is important that: (1) you establish what the potential decisions are at your university; and (2) you genuinely understand what these terms mean.

Decisions can be any of the following:

- Degree awarded.
- Degree awarded subject to corrections to satisfy internal examiner.
- Thesis to be resubmitted, according to recommendations, within X months.
- Thesis to be resubmitted after further research within X months.
- Degree not awarded.
- Degree not awarded. Master degree awarded.

By far the most common outcome is a 'pass with revisions'. This is not to be construed as a fail. If you complete the required revisions by the stated deadline, you will graduate.

At the end of the day, there may not be a great difference between the original and the revised thesis. In fact, some experienced supervisors would go as far as saying that they do not believe that a revised thesis is much better than the original. Even the third level of decision, requiring further research or more substantial revision, is still close to a pass, assuming that the additional work can be done. Even the requirement for a second oral examination, while discouraging, is not an outright fail. Finally, 'Degree awarded' without revisions and the outright fail of 'Degree not awarded' are relatively rare.

Revisions and corrections

The purpose of revisions and corrections is, of course, to strengthen the argument and improve presentation and literary style, where needed. The key point for students is to be sure exactly what is expected in terms of revisions or corrections.

Most examiners will present a typed list of corrections to the student. Well-prepared students will already have made their own list and may already have corrected typos and other minor errors. If, however, you are asked to note down the required revisions, be sure to reflect back your notes and summaries in order to confirm your understanding and secure agreement. For example, if the examiner asks you for 'a bit more on' a topic, is he or she expecting you to write a sentence or two, or a page or several pages? Revisions are much easier to do when the task is defined precisely.

It is important to distinguish revisions that aim to improve the work and those that are intended to improve the text. At this stage, most will be about strengthening the argument and therefore this discussion will focus on matters of text.

It is worth remembering that the examiner may propose certain revisions in order to strengthen a piece of work that is already very strong; in other words, revisions are not necessarily a sign of failure. It may be that revisions will increase the credibility of a piece of work and its potential for impact in practice or publication.

There are many different types of revision, from minor to major:

- expanding on some aspect of the work;
- making decisions more transparent;
- increasing documentation of steps, decisions and analysis;
- adjusting conceptual leaps;
- removing 'smoothing' of results;
- reinstating discrepancies;
- writing new sections;
- modulating generalizations that diminish the power of the data and/or analysis;
- improving the match between the study, the conclusions and the recommendations.

Revisions are intended to strengthen the argument of the thesis. Some can involve reinstating sections that you removed earlier, thinking that you were strengthening the thesis. New researchers often do not dare to leave gaps or discrepancies. However, every piece of research has its gaps and indeterminacies; it would be unusual if there were none in your analysis, for example. In fact, these are often an important dimension of the research. If you have saved deleted sections, it will be simple enough to replace them. Clearly, the whole research process cannot be transparent, or the thesis would be thousands of pages long, but the examiner may want you to adjust the balance of what went in and what went out of the thesis.

This may be one of the things that you cannot really see clearly until the end of the process. In preparing for the examination, you should be realizing how much of the doctoral process, and theoretically the examination process, is about the journey you have taken. You start out with little or no experience of a major research project and travel towards your destination, learning many lessons along the way. Your perspective on your work and your thesis may be completely different when you reach this point.

When revisions are finally proposed, it is important that they are defined:

Questions about revisions

- Is your task clear?
- Is it necessary? The point they are looking for may already be covered in another chapter.
- Can you negotiate?
- Is each revision specific: length, content, placing? Could it be more defined?
- Can you do this?
- Will you need help and resources?
- Do you have a deadline?
- Can you do the revisions immediately?
- How will the supervisor support you during revisions?

There may be an overlap between what the examiner sees as potential developments of your work and what they want you to develop in your revisions. You may have to clarify – and confirm – this at some stage during the discussion.

Where supervisors are permitted to attend a doctoral examination, they can, of course, provide a useful extra level of 'interpretation' of the examiner's requirements. Even if they are not present at the examination, supervisors may be invited to participate in discussions of such changes. However, this does not mean that they are responsible for them; that responsibility rests with the candidate.

If the examiner promises to forward the text of their recommendations for revisions to you, try to secure a date for this. It has been known for examiners – and candidates – to disappear for months after the examination, especially if there is a holiday around this time. Arrange a meeting to discuss the proposed revisions with your supervisor as soon as possible. This will allow you to check your understanding and help you to get started on your final phase of work.

Sometimes students set off to do more substantive revisions than are required and your supervisor may be able to help you make the changes as economically as possible. On the other hand, you would presumably prefer to avoid doing the opposite: too little. Again, you should look to your supervisor for advice. This might require careful discussion, rather than just a quick question-and-answer phone call or e-mail.

Once you have completed your minor revisions and/or corrections you usually have to submit them to the internal examiner – you should have been told whom to submit them to and what will happen once you have after your examination. If not, or if you have forgotten, check with your supervisor. Usually, the external examiner is only involved in this phase when major revisions are required. It is not your supervisor who will do the final checking. In order to help your examiner to see your revisions you might think of marking them in some way. It might also be helpful to submit a photocopy of the changes requested along with the final copy.

Appeals

If you feel you have been treated unfairly in your examination, you may want to appeal. You should check your university's grounds for appeal after an examination. All universities have written explanations of appeals processes, possibly in their codes of practice. Explanations should include potential grounds for an appeal. These may – or may not – include:

- procedural irregularities in the conduct of the examination;
- medical or personal (or, in some cases, other) circumstances affecting a student's performance, of which the examiners were unaware when they made their decision about the outcome;
- prejudice or bias on the part of the examiner(s).

Appeals are usually made to the university senate or board, although they might first go through a graduate school committee.

Rudd (1985) identified reasons why students he interviewed thought that they had grounds for appeal. Based on this research, he produced what he considered to be grounds for an appeal:

- ideological differences between students and staff leading to unfair treatment at the examination;
- supervisor error;
- supervisor failure to alert the student to significant weaknesses in the early stages of the work;
- examiner's personal hostility towards the student.

'Fairness' was Rudd's focus in his chapter on the doctoral examination. How-ever, he acknowledged how difficult it would be for students to make a case that they had been treated unfairly:

> The only kinds of appeal open to a PhD candidate are those that are gener-ally open to any student with a grievance . . . [which] are of little use to the aggrieved PhD student, as he would find it almost impossible to prove that he had been unfairly treated. Also a legal action is apt to be expensive.
>
> (Rudd 1985: 113)

After all, he points out, the examination is all about *subjective* assessment by one person, the external examiner, and Rudd goes on to infer that a different group of examiners might reach a different decision. However, this is not to say that students who receive a negative result should automatically appeal. The university's grounds for appeal must be the student's guide.

Wakeford (2002: 35) supplies a similar, more recent, warning:

> One student is pursuing his appeal on the grounds that after the viva the internal had informed him that he had been allocated the wrong supervisor at the start. But, aware of the tradition of academic patronage, most of these students feared that submitting an appeal would further jeopardise their careers. Being 'in dispute' with one's university can mean precisely that. It is either 'you' or 'they' who will be the winner. Unfortunately, it is 'they' who enjoy the privilege of inventing the rules and holding all the cards, so it starts off as a very unequal battle. What is more, the institution will have an intimate familiarity with its own appeal procedures and how they operate; for the student, the experience of an appeal will be a novel and potentially traumatic one, with everything to be gained or lost.

The validity of Rudd's and Wakeford's findings depends on the accuracy and honesty of student accounts of their experiences. However, even with that reservation, Wakeford argues that there are grounds for an inquiry – if not an appeal – in some of the cases he cites.

Rudd proposed in 1985 that an appeal should lead to remarking of a thesis by a panel of experts who are not aware that the thesis has been failed. It is an interesting idea, but how would that be managed and resourced? It may be, of course, that such practices are already in place in some universities. It is worth checking.

Check your institution

The key question is, what are the grounds for appeal at your institution?

'Universities', in general, know their procedures better than students. Taking the university to court is an expensive process. However, if there were circumstances that the examiners did not know about, that affected your performance, you might be able to argue the case.

Needless to say, appeals that are directly concerned with the procedures and practices of the examination itself, as opposed to complaints about the supervisor, for example, are more easily dealt with if the examination that is the subject of the appeal had a chairperson present. The chair can act as an independent witness. This is why many institutions are now moving towards the practice of including some type of independent witness in all doctoral examinations.

Recovery

The days after the viva were black ones. It was like having a severe accident. For the first few hours I was numbed, unable to realize what had hit me. Then I began to wonder if I would make a recovery and win through.

(Gordon 1952: 173)

You may find, as many students have in the past, that you feel exhausted and even emotional after your examination. Even an examination that lasts only two hours can be a draining experience, since it draws on so many different skills. Expect to feel drained. Plan activities that will help you to recover.

Celebrations

Take time to celebrate with those who have helped and supported you. If they seem more pleased about your result than you, try to go along with that spirit. You may have to pretend, but you can privately consider it part of your thank you to them.

Anti-climax

It was like coming out of a doctor's surgery after being told that what looked like something nasty on the x-ray was only some coffee spilled on the film.

(Sale 2001: 9)

Having focused your whole life – or much of it – on achieving this one goal, now that you have achieved it, there is no focus, for a moment, or a month, or for longer. This can be a confusing time. Even if you do plan your recovery well, you can expect to feel a mixture of positive and negative emotions:

> My feelings ... were those of a private unexpectedly promoted to a general overnight. In a minute or two I had been transformed from an unearning and potentially dishonest ragamuffin to a respectable and solvent member of a learned profession.
>
> (Gordon 1952: 184)

> You may expect that you will feel only relief and pleasure when you earn your degree, so you may be startled by feelings of loss and sadness.
>
> (Bolker 1998: 127)

> Maybe you will grieve that a major stage of your life is over, or perhaps you will mourn the important people who are not alive to witness your triumph, or maybe you'll confront the gap between the dissertation you've actually written and the one you imagined you would write ... Every major life change destroys the equilibrium of our lives and our self-image and leaves behind a portion of an old self.
>
> (Bolker 1998: 127–8)

You may even feel depressed. This will only confuse you, of course, if you were expecting unadulterated joy and relief.

You have made so many sacrifices – as have your friends, family and loved ones – there is no immediate benefit to you – or to them – as a result of your passing the examination.

The examination itself may not have been as challenging as you expected. You may feel that you wasted your time in over-preparing for something that turned out to be a routine discussion among scholars.

> Little shreds of success collected together and weaved themselves into a triumphal garland ... For about three days the world is at your feet, then you realize it's the beginning, not the end. You've got to fight a damn sight harder than you did in your exams to do your job decently and make a living.
>
> (Gordon 1952: 173–4, 187)

In the midst of this flux of feelings you have to construct your own sense of closure, even when you still have a little or a lot more work to do to revise the thesis. At the very least, you can start planning for graduation.

Endnote for students

No one will ever ask you about your performance at the event at which [your thesis] was accepted.

(Bolker 1998: 134)

You may find yourself realizing during the examination how far you have come from when you started. You may find yourself thinking that what matters is not so much what you produced in your research or what you wrote in your thesis, but the journey you made in the course of your study. The examination is a test of how far you have travelled. It is an interrogation of how you see the journey. Above all, it may be the first time that you realize this.

In all your preparations, and in all the advice provided in this book, the emphasis has been on performance, yet once the examination is over, that performance evaporates. In the years to come people will ask you what you studied for your doctorate, and perhaps where and with whom, but they will not ask you, 'How did you do in your oral examination?' Whether this is because no one really wants to know or because no one dares to ask is an interesting question. However, the fact remains that once it is over, it is over. Move on.

Bibliography

Allpress, B. and Barnacle, R. (2009) Projecting the PhD: architectural design research by and through projects, in D. Boud and A. Lee (eds), *Changing Practices of Doctoral Education*. London: Routledge, pp. 157–70.

Bain, S. A. and Baxter, J. S. (2000) Interrogative suggestibility: the role of interviewer behaviour, *Legal and Criminal Psychology*, 5: 123–33.

Baldacchino, G. (1995) Reflections on the status of a doctoral defence, *Journal of Graduate Education*, 1: 71–6.

Baldick, C. (1990) *The Concise Oxford Dictionary of Literary Terms*. Oxford: Oxford University Press.

Bolker, J. (1998) *Writing Your Dissertation in Fifteen Minutes a Day: A Guide to Starting, Revising and Finishing Your Doctoral Thesis*. New York: Henry Holt.

Boud, D. and Lee, A. (2009) *Changing Practices of Doctoral Education*. London: Routledge.

Brause, R. S. (2000) *Writing Your Doctoral Dissertation: Invisible Rules for Success*. London: Falmer.

Brennan, J., Williams, R., Harris, R. and McNamara, D. (1997) An institutional approach to quality audit, *Studies in Higher Education*, 22(2): 173–86.

British Psychological Society (2000) *Guidelines for Assessment of the PhD in Psychology and Related Disciplines*, revised version. Leicester: British Psychological Society.

Brown, G. and Atkins, M. (1988) *Effective Teaching in Higher Education*. London: Routledge.

Burnham, P. (1994) Surviving the viva: unravelling the mystery of the PhD oral, *Journal of Graduate Education*, 1: 30–4.

Caffarella, R. S. and Barnett, B. G. (2000) Teaching doctoral students to become scholarly writers: the importance of giving and receiving critiques, *Studies in Higher Education*, 25(1): 39–51.

Carless, D. R. (2002) The 'mini-viva' as a tool to enhance assessment for learning, *Assessment and Evaluation in Higher Education*, 27(4): 353–63.

Christensen, C. R., Garvin, D. A. and Sweet, A. (eds) (1991) *Education for Judgement: The Artistry of Discussion Leadership*. Boston: Harvard Business School.

Delamont, S. (1998) Creating a delicate balance: the doctoral supervisor's dilemma, *Teaching in Higher Education*, 3(2): 157–72.

Delamont, S., Atkinson, P. and Parry, O. (1997) *Supervising the PhD: A Guide to Success*. Buckingham: Society for Research into Higher Education and Open University Press.

Delamont, S., Atkinson, P. and Parry, O. (2000) *The Doctoral Experience: Success and Failure in Graduate School*. London: Falmer.

Doncaster, K. and Thorne, L. (2000) Reflection and planning: essential elements of professional doctorates, *Reflective Practice*, 1(3): 391–9.

Droogleever Fortuyn, H. A., van Broekhoven, F., Span, P. N., Bäckström, F. G. and Verkes,

J. (2004) Effects of PhD examination stress on allopregnanolone and cortisol plasma levels and peripheral benzodiazepine receptor density, *Psychoneuroendocrinology*, 29(10): 1341–4.

Eley, A. and Murray, R. (2009) *How to Be an Effective Supervisor*. Maidenhead: Open University Press.

Evans, T. and Kamler, B. (2002) Doctoral theses: risky representations and the problems for examination, in E. McWilliam (ed.), *Research Training for the Knowledge Economy*. Proceedings of the 4th International Biennial Conference on Professional Doctorates. Brisbane: Queensland University of Technology.

Gardner, S. K. (2008) 'What's too much and what's too little?: The process of becoming an independent researcher in doctoral education, *Journal of Higher Education*, 79(3): 326–351.

Gordon, R. (1952) *Doctor in the House*. Harmondsworth: Penguin.

Graves, N. (1997) *Working for a Doctorate*. London: Routledge.

Green, D. H. (1998) *The Postgraduate Viva: A Closer Look* (video). Leeds: Leeds Metropolitan University.

Hartley, J. (2000) Nineteen ways to have a viva, *Psychology Postgraduate Affairs Group Quarterly Newsletter*, 35: 22–8.

Hartley, J. and Fox, C. (2002) The viva experience: examining the examiners, *Higher Education Review*, 35(1), 24–30.

Hartley, J. and Fox, C. (2004) Assessing the mock viva: the experiences of British doctoral students, *Studies in Higher Education*, 29(6): 727–38.

Hartley, J. and Jory, S. (2000a) Lifting the veil on the viva: the experiences of psychology PhD candidates in the UK, *Psychology Teaching Review*, 9(2): 76–90.

Hartley, J. and Jory, S. (2000b) Experiencing the viva: the implications of students' views, *Psychology Postgraduate Affairs Group Quarterly Newsletter*, September, 19–25.

Hockey, J. (1994) New territory: problems of adjusting to the first year of a social science PhD, *Studies in Higher Education*, 19(2): 177–90.

Hoddell, S., Street, D. and Wildblood, H. (2002) Doctorates – converging or diverging patterns of provision?, *Quality Assurance in Education*, 19(2): 61–70.

Holbrook, A., Bourke, S., Fairbairn, H. and Lovat, T. (2007) Examiner comment on the literature review in Ph.D. theses, *Studies in Higher Education*, 32(3): 337–56.

Jackson, C. and Tinkler, P. (2000) The PhD examination: an exercise in community building and gatekeeping? In I. McNay (ed.) *Higher Education and its Communities*. Buckingham: Society for Research into Higher Education and Open University Press.

Jackson, C. and Tinkler, P. (2001) Back to basics: a consideration of the purposes of the PhD viva, *Assessment and Evaluation in Higher Education*, 26(4): 354–66.

Jackson, C. and Tinkler, P. (2007) *A Guide for Internal and External Examiners*. London: Society for Research into Higher Education.

Johnston, S. (1997) Examining the examiners: an analysis of examiners' reports on doctoral theses, *Studies in Higher Education*, 22(3): 333–47.

Kerlin, B. (1998) The pursuit of the PhD: is it good for your health? (http://kerlin.net/bobbi/research/health.html).

Leonard, D. (2001) *A Woman's Guide to Doctoral Studies*. Buckingham: Open University Press.

Levine, S. J. (2002) Writing and presenting your thesis or dissertation (http://www.learnerassociates.net/dissthes/#30).

Loumansky, A. and Jackson, S. (2004) Out of the frying pan into the viva, *Journal of International Women's Studies*, 5(3): 22–32.

Mansfield, N. (2008) *The Final Hurdle: A Guide to a Successful Viva*. London: Royal Society of Chemistry.

Metcalfe, J., Thompson, Q. and Green, H. (2002) Improving standards in postgraduate research degree programmes. Higher Education Funding Council for England (http://www.hefce.ac.uk/pubs/Rdreports/summary/summ13.htm).

Morgan, A. (2002) Examine the logic (letter), *Times Higher Education Supplement*, 9 August: 13.

Morley, L., Leonard, D. and David, M. (2002) Variations in vivas: quality and equality in British PhD assessments, *Studies in Higher Education*, 27(3): 263–73.

Morss, K. and Murray, R. (2005) *Teaching at University: A Handbook for Postgraduates and Researchers*. London: Sage.

Mullins, G. and Kiley, M. (2002) 'It's a PhD, not a Nobel Prize': how experienced examiners assess research theses, *Studies in Higher Education*, 27(4): 369–86.

Murray, R. (1998) *The Viva* (video and notes). Glasgow: University of Strathclyde.

Murray, R. (2003a) Students' questions and their implications for the viva, *Quality Assurance in Education*, 11(2): 109–13.

Murray, R. (2003b) Survive your Viva, *Guardian*: September 16.

Murray, R. (2006) *How to Write a Thesis*, 2nd edn. Buckingham: Open University Press.

National Postgraduate Committee (1992) *Guidelines on Codes of Practice for Postgraduate Research*. Nottingham: NPC.

National Postgraduate Committee (1995) *Guidelines for the Conduct of Research Degree Appeals*. Nottingham: NPC.

Newberry, D. (1995) A journey in research from research assistant to doctor of philosophy, *Journal of Graduate Education*, 2: 53–9.

Partington, J., Brown, G. and Gordon, G. (1993) *Handbook for External Examiners in Higher Education*. Sheffield: UK Universities' Staff Development Unit and the Universities of Kent and Leeds.

Patton, M. Q. (1982) *Practical Evaluation*. London: Sage.

Pearce, L. (2005) *How to Examine a Thesis*. Maidenhead: Open University Press.

Pearson, M. and Brew, A. (2002) Research training and supervision development, *Studies in Higher Education*, 27(2): 135–50.

Phillips, E. M. and Pugh, D. S. (2000) *How to Get a PhD: A Handbook for Students and their Supervisors*, 3rd edn. Buckingham: Open University Press.

Pitt, M. (1999) A doctoral viva by videoconference. In W. Alexander, C. Higgison and N. Mogey (eds) *Videoconferencing in Teaching and Learning*. Edinburgh: Learning Technology Dissemination Initiative and TALiSMAN.

Potter, S. (ed.) (2002) *Doing Postgraduate Research*. London: Sage.

Powell, S. and Brown, K. (2007) *Access to Doctoral Examiners' Reports*. Lichfield: UK Council for Graduate Education.

Quality Assurance Agency (1999) *Code of Practice for the Assurance of Academic Quality and Standards in Higher Education: Postgraduate Research Programmes*. Gloucester: Quality Assurance Agency for Higher Education.

Radice, E. (1971) *Who's Who in the Ancient World: A Handbook to the Survivors of the Greek and Roman Classics*. Harmondsworth: Penguin.

Rudd, E. (1985) *A New Look at Postgraduate Failure*. Guildford: Society for Research in Higher Education, NFER/Nelson.

Ruggeri-Stevens, G., Bareham, J. and Bourner, T. (2001) The DBA in British universities: assessment and standards, *Quality Assurance in Education*, 9(2): 61–71.

Ryan, Y. and Zuber-Skerritt, O. (1999) *Supervising Postgraduates from Non-English Speaking*

Backgrounds. Buckingham: Society for Research into Higher Education and Open University Press.

Sale, J. (2001) The PhD gave me cunning, *Independent*, Education Supplement, 27 September: 9.

Sarros, J. C., Willis, R. J., Fisher, R. and Storen, A. (2005) DBA examination procedures and protocols, *Journal of Higher Education Policy and Management*, 27(2): 151–72.

Sartre, J-P. (1945) *Huis Clos*. Paris: Gallimard.

Scott, D., Brown, A., Lunt, I. and Thorne, L. (2004) *Professional Doctorates: Integrating Professional and Academic Knowledge*. Maidenhead: Open University Press.

Shaw, F. (1997) *Out of Me: The Story of a Postnatal Breakdown*. London: Penguin.

Snow, C. P. (1960) *The Affair*. London: Reprint Society.

Stephens, D. (2001) Why I . . . believe all PhD students should be grilled in public, *Times Higher Education Supplement*, 20 April: 16.

Swift, J. and Douglas, A. (1997) *The Viva Voce*. Birmingham: Birmingham Institute of Art and Design.

Tannen, D. (1995) *Talking from 9 to 5: How Men's and Women's Conversational Styles Affect who Gets Heard, who Gets Credit, and what Gets Done at Work*. London: Virago.

Tinkler, P. and Jackson, C. (2000) Examining the doctorate: institutional policy and the PhD examination process in Britain, *Studies in Higher Education*, 25(2): 167–80.

Tinkler, P. and Jackson, C. (2004) *The Doctoral Examination Process: A Handbook for Students, Examiners and Supervisors*. Buckingham: Society for Research into Higher Education and Open University Press.

Trafford, V. and Leshem, S. (2002a) Anatomy of a doctoral viva, *Journal of Graduate Education*, 3: 33–41.

Trafford, V. and Leshem, S. (2002b) Starting at the end to undertake doctoral research: predictable questions as stepping stones, *Higher Education Review*, 35(1): 31–49.

Trafford, V. and Leshem, S. (2008) *Stepping Stones to Achieving your Doctorate: By Focusing on your Viva from the Start*. Maidenhead: Open University Press.

Trafford, V., Woolliams, P. and Leshem, S. (2002) Dynamics of the doctoral viva. Paper presented at the UK Council for Graduate Education Summer Conference, University of Gloucestershire, 15–16 July.

Universities' and Colleges' Staff Development Agency (UCoSDA) (1993) *Handbook for External Examiners in Higher Education*. Sheffield: UCoSDA and Committee of Vice-Chancellors and Principals of the Universities of the United Kingdom.

Usher, R. (2002) A diversity of doctorates: fitness for the knowledge economy?, *Higher Education Research and Development*, 21(2): 143–53.

Wakeford, J. (2002) What goalposts?, *Guardian*, Education section, 17 September: 35. (See also readers' responses at http://education.guardian.co.uk.).

Wakeford, J. (2009) PhD Diaries: an archive of accounts of their experiences by doctoral students, supervisors and examiners. http://www.ucl.ac.uk/calt/phd-diaries/index.php#db.

Walker, G. E., Golde, C. M., Bueschel, C. and Hutchings, P. (2008) *The Formation of Scholars: Rethinking Doctoral Education for the Twenty-First Century*. San Francisco: Jossey-Bass.

Winter, R., Griffiths, M. and Green, K. (2000) The 'academic' qualities of practice: what are the criteria for a practice-based PhD?, *Studies in Higher Education*, 25(1): 25–37.

Wisker, G. (2001) *The Postgraduate Research Handbook*. Basingstoke: Palgrave.

Zuber-Skerrit, O. and Ryan, Y. (eds) (1994) *Quality in Postgraduate Education*. London: Kogan Page.

Index

Related books from Open University Press
Purchase from www.openup.co.uk or order through your local bookseller

STEPPING STONES TO ACHIEVING YOUR DOCTORATE
FOCUSING ON YOUR VIVA FROM THE START

Vernon Trafford and Shosh Leshem

- What criteria are used to assess the scholarly merit of a thesis?
- What is the level of conceptualization that is expected in doctoral theses?
- How can you prepare to defend your thesis?
- What is the most effective route to achieving your doctorate?

The starting point to achieving your doctorate is to appreciate how your thesis will be examined. The criteria that examiners use, the questions they ask in vivas and their reports provide templates against which theses are judged. So, why not start from this endpoint as you plan, undertake, write and defend your research?

This book focuses specifically on how you, as a doctoral candidate, can raise your level of thinking about your chosen topic. Doing so will improve the quality of your research and ultimately contribute to knowledge. It also explores the nature of conceptualization which is sought by examiners in theses. As a candidate, the book provides those essential characteristics of doctorateness that examiners expect to find in your thesis.

The book will also appeal to supervisors, examiners and those who conduct workshops for doctoral candidates and supervisors.

This practical book includes extracts from theses, examiner reports and cameo accounts from doctoral examiners, supervisors and candidates. It also contains numerous visual models that explain relationships and processes for you to apply and use in your doctoral journey.

Based upon contemporary practice, Stepping Stones to Achieving your Doctorate is an essential tool for doctoral candidates, supervisors and examiners.

Contents

List of examples – List of figures – List of tables – List of tasks – Acknowledgements – Introduction – The end is where we start from – What is doctorateness? – Architecture of the doctoral thesis – Exploiting the literature – Thinking about research design – Whats in a word? – How to conclude your thesis in one chapter – The abstract – The magic circle: Putting it all together – Preparing for the viva – Dynamics of the doctoral viva – Epilogue: Arriving back at where we started – References – Index – Author name index.

2008   264pp
978-0-335-22543-9 (Paperback)   978-0-335-22542-2 (Hardback)

HOW TO GET A PhD 4e
A HANDBOOK FOR STUDENTS AND THEIR SUPERVISORS
Estelle M. Phillips and Derek S. Pugh

Reviews of the third edition:

> This remains the best general . . . introduction to working on the PhD. It is well worth consulting by anyone considering the PhD as a route to take, either part-time combined with employment, or full time as a route into academia.
>
> *Social Research Association*

> This is an excellent book. Its style is racy and clear . . . an impressive array of information, useful advice and comment gleaned from the authors' systematic study and experience over many years . . . should be required reading not only for those contemplating doctoral study but also for supervisors, new and experienced.
>
> *Higher Education*

Since the first edition of this innovative book appeared in 1987 it has become a world-wide bestseller. Through it many thousands of students in all faculties and disciplines have been helped to gain their PhDs.

Practical and clear, this book examines everything students need to know about getting a PhD through research in any subject. It also helps supervisors and examiners to better understand their role in the process.

New to this edition:

- Completely updated throughout
- New section on increasingly popular professional doctorates such as EdD, DBA and D.Eng
- New material for overseas, part-time and mature students, and their supervisors
- New diagnostic questionnaire for students to self-monitor progress
- Takes in the impact of the new Code of Practice of the Quality Assurance Agency

Includes stories of other PhD students, problems they encountered and how they dealt with them!

How to get a PhD is the essential handbook for doctoral students!

Contents

Preface to the fourth edition – On becoming a research student – Getting into the system – The nature of the PhD qualification – How not to get a PhD – How to do research – The form of a PhD thesis – The PhD process – How to manage your supervisors – How to survive in a predominantly British, white, male, full-time, heterosexual academic environment – The examination system – How to supervise and examine – Institutional responsibilities – Appendix – References – Index.

2005   240pp
978–0–335–21684–0 (Paperback)   978–0–335–21685–7 (Hardback)